on
war

Bernard Shaw
on
war

edited by J.P. Wearing

ET REMOTISSIMA PROPE

'on'

'on'
Published by Hesperus Press Limited
4 Rickett Street, London sw6 1ru
www.hesperuspress.com

Bernard Shaw texts: © 2009 The Trustees of the British Museum,
the Governors and Guardians of the National Gallery of Ireland,
and Royal Academy of Dramatic Art
First published by Hesperus Press Limited, 2009

This edition edited by J.P. Wearing
Introduction, editorial matter and selection © J.P. Wearing, 2009
Foreword © Philip Pullman, 2009

Designed and typeset by Fraser Muggeridge studio
Printed in Jordan by Jordan National Press

ISBN: 978-1-84391-611-6

Contents

Foreword

Bernard Shaw was born in the last year of the Crimean War, the most famous engagement of which, the Charge of the Light Brigade, involved mounted cavalry; by the time he died, the world was already five years into the age of the atom bomb. The ninety-four years of his lifetime have a fair claim to be the most warlike period in human history – certainly the one in which more blood was spilled than any other. The American Civil War, the Franco-Prussian War, the Boer War, the Russo-Japanese War, the Spanish Civil War, the two great world wars, not to mention the various revolutions, in Russia and elsewhere, which involved armed struggle and conflict – the list goes on and on. It would be surprising if a writer with such inexhaustible curiosity about human affairs did not have something to say about this most sombre yet most thrilling of subjects. War is a central concern of several of his plays, from *Arms and the Man* to *The Devil's Disciple* to *Major Barbara* to *Heartbreak House* to *Saint Joan*; in pamphlets, speeches, books and letters he returned to the subject again and again.

And, being Shaw, he annoyed people intensely. The common complaint about Shaw, common at any rate among those who don't like him, is most vividly expressed in the famous description by W.B. Yeats of his reaction to *Arms and the Man*: 'It seemed to me inorganic, logical straightness and not the crooked road of life, yet I stood aghast before its energy... Presently I had a nightmare that I was haunted by a sewing-machine, that clicked and shone, but the incredible thing was that the machine smiled, smiled perpetually.'

The bloodless, sexless, endlessly talking puppet who cut intellectual capers and spouted brilliant nonsense: that was the GBS who was his own most popular invention. He had to make people laugh, he explained, or they would stone him for telling the truth, and the truth was what he strove most assiduously to tell in his pamphlet of 1914, *Common Sense About the War*. From the distance of nearly a century, we can find much to agree with, not least his clear-sighted view of the consequences as far as working people were concerned: 'I ask the heavens, with a shudder, do these class-blinded people in authority really intend to take a million men out of their employment; turn them into soldiers; and then at one blow hurl them back, utterly unprovided for, into the streets?'

And his view from 1914 of the likely outcome of the conflict was realised in the Treaty of Versailles five years later, almost exactly as he had foreseen: 'We had better not say to the Kaiser at the end of the war, "Scoundrel: you can never replace the Louvain Library, nor the sculpture of Rheims; and it follows logically that you shall empty your pockets into ours." Much better say: "God forgive us all!" If we cannot rise to this, and must soil our hands with plunder, at least let us call it plunder, and not profane our language and our souls by giving it fine names.'

For this, and the rest of the Shavian common sense so vividly and generously on display in *Common Sense About the War*, he was roundly abused by almost everyone. H.G. Wells complained in the *Daily Chronicle* that Shaw was 'an elderly adolescent still at play… All through the war we shall have this Shavian accompaniment going on, like an idiot child screaming in a hospital.' And the playwright Henry Arthur Jones was moved to a pitch of frenzy: 'The hag Sedition was your mother, and Perversity begot you… no other ancestry and rearing had you, you freakish homunculus, germinated outside of lawful procreation.'

Shaw's even-tempered good humour in the face of attacks like this was, of course, one of the things that people found most infuriating, not to say inhuman, about him. It was no doubt easier to regard him simply as a clown, a maker of glittering comedy, than to take him seriously. One of his very first plays, *Arms and the Man*, shows that comic brilliance already at work in the old soldier Bluntschli who carries chocolate instead of bullets in his cartridge-case, undermining the romantic dreams of heroism expressed by the woman in whose bedroom he has taken refuge.

The greatest quality of his plays, however, is not their wit but the way in which that wit is used in the service of intellectual exposition. Shaw could dramatise argument as well as any playwright who ever lived, and it's that sense of thrilling and desperate hand-to-hand rhetorical combat that permeates the best of his work for the theatre. That is what keeps his plays alive, as recent National Theatre productions of *Saint Joan* and *Major Barbara* have shown. His preoccupations, as given shape in those plays alone, could hardly be more relevant to the present age: the arms trade, the inexorable quality of capitalism, the strange ways in which religion and war can become entwined.

This selection from his plays and other works is rich in the passages that demand to be included, and surprising in others. I had never seen the fable he wrote in 1916 for a Belgian children's charity, with its strangely J.M. Barrie-like atmosphere. There are not many children in Shaw's work, and given the faintly unwholesome nursery-nostalgia that pervades so much that was written for or about the young in the early years of the twentieth century, perhaps it's just as well: even this piece is not entirely free of it. However, for the most part Shaw had the bracing and healthy notion that grown-up preoccupations were more interesting than childish ones, and that the more grown-up we were the better it would be for the world; *Back to Methuselah* is all about that very idea.

But one of the most interesting things about Shaw, and the one I admire most, is the depth of his feeling and the genuine kindness that are entirely overlooked by those who dismiss him as a cold-blooded and facetious windbag. To see those best qualities at their most intense, we have to go to the letters, and the letter in this selection, to Mrs Patrick Campbell on the death of her son, can stand for many more. Nothing in the least of false comfort, or sentimental consolation: just plain blazing anger, and all the more human for that.

Shaw told the truth about war, as he did about many subjects. He was wrong about some things; he was wrong about Stalin and the Soviet Union, though he had Hitler's number; but he was one of the greatest enemies that *cant* ever had, and even Yeats, of the nightmarish sewing-machine that smiled and smiled, went on to say that Shaw 'could hit my enemies and the enemies of all I loved, as I could never hit.' And he wrote with a classic and beautiful clarity that has the power to lift the spirits like champagne, even when we disagree with him. As time goes by, perhaps that will come to be seen as his greatest quality of all.

– *Philip Pullman, 2009*

Introduction

Writing in 1945, Shaw looked back to the Franco-Prussian war of 1870–1: 'I was fifteen at the time, and remember it quite well.'[1] His recollection is particularly significant because Germany's defeat of France in 1871 marked a shift in the balance of European power as a unified Germany supplanted France as the dominant force on the continent. Germany's victory also laid the groundwork for the subsequent world wars that eventually brought about yet another reconfiguration of military power. Shaw's lifetime encompassed several other conflicts, such as the two Boer Wars (1880–1, 1899–1902) and the Spanish Civil War (1936–9); just months before his death in 1950, the Korean War broke out. Moreover, Shaw knew war in an era that saw an exponential growth in the potential for carnage, from the cavalry charge and sabres to the atomic bomb.

Enterprisingly, Shaw made war the focus of his first commercially produced play, *Arms and the Man* (1894), which evokes two wars: the brief Serbo-Bulgarian War (1885–6) and the Crimean War (1854–6), the latter remembered for the charge of the Light Brigade at the Battle of Balaclava. The play subverts Victorian jingoism as a realistic Swiss mercenary, Bluntschli, exposes the romantic, idealistic illusions about war and battle entertained by the Byronic figure, Sergius (pp.3–5). *Arms and the Man* is typical of Shaw's approach to the subject of war since it branches out to cover other topics, such as class structure and marriage. In fact, Shaw could never confine himself to a single topic, but was compelled to exhaust virtually every nuance and ramification his fertile and controversial mind could find.

The fictional Bluntschli is a more modest figure than the historical militarists Shaw depicted in several other plays: Napoleon in *The Man of Destiny* (1897), Julius Caesar in *Caesar and Cleopatra* (1901), the eponymous Saint Joan (1923), or the trio of dictators (Mussolini, Hitler, and Franco) in *Geneva* (1938).

However, the shrewd, lowly soldier, who reappears in *O'Flaherty, V.C.* (1917), intrigued Shaw the socialist who saw war, class, and capitalism as being linked inextricably. In an 1891 Fabian pamphlet, *The Impossibilities of Anarchism*, Shaw wrote, 'Your soldier, ostensibly a heroic and patriotic defender of his country, is really an unfortunate man driven by destitution to offer himself as food for powder for the sake of regular rations, shelter and clothing; and he must, on pain of being arbitrarily imprisoned, punished with petty penances like a naughty child, pack-drilled, flogged or shot, all in the blessed name of "discipline," do anything he is ordered to.' Shaw's pamphlet further criticised England's class-ridden social hierarchy of which the soldier was but an inferior member. He took up the soldier's cause in another Fabian manifesto, *Fabianism and the Empire* (1900), written to gloss the Fabians' divided stance on the second Boer War. Shaw declared soldiers were entitled to 'full civil rights', 'a living wage', guaranteed employment until retirement age, 'and then an adequate pension'. Officers too needed to meet high professional standards and be paid accordingly. Shaw's personal view of the war was expressed more forthrightly in two private letters written in 1899 and 1900 in which he declared that the two warring parties were indistinguishable, and that he was interested only in how socialism might benefit from the outcome (The Boer War and The Boer War Revisited, pp.6–8).

Despite some of the sentiments in his 1900 letter, Shaw was not a pacifist, as his friend G.K. Chesterton pointed out in 1910: 'Shaw only objects to [wars] in so far as they are ideal; that is in so far as they are idealised. Shaw objects not so much to war as to the attractiveness of war… Shaw merely murmurs, "Wars if you must; but for God's sake, not war songs."'[2] Indeed, waging war as a fundamental human characteristic is the central point of the Devil's lively speech in *Man and Superman* (pp.8–10).

What makes modern warfare ever more destructive are the advances in weaponry and the ability of industrialists to produce weapons and explosives for increasing numbers of ready buyers.

Undershaft in *Major Barbara* (1905) is one such amoral weapons manufacturer, a predecessor of that dominant global economic force – the military-industrial complex (pp.10–12). During the play, Shaw enlarges his theme by paradoxically comparing Undershaft's success in achieving model living and working conditions for his munitions workers with his daughter Barbara's unsuccessful attempts at aiding the poor, weak, and hungry through the Salvation Army's charitable efforts.

In the years preceding 1914, Shaw 'knew that all the parties were up to the neck in Balance of Power diplomacy as laid down in Machiavelli's famous treatise [*The Prince*],' spurred on by the growth of Germany's navy and the threat it posed. Countries sought to mitigate threats by striking various alliances or agreements, such as the Anglo-French *entente cordiale* signed in 1904 chiefly as a result of French fears about Germany. Shaw's response was his proposal in 1913 for a series of interlocking alliances to prevent war (pp.12–13). Not unexpectedly, his warning proved futile; existing alliances and Germany's violation of Belgian neutrality in August 1914 led to Britain's declaration of war.

The outbreak of the Great War found Shaw on holiday, but he immediately began writing *Common Sense About the War* (pp.13–27), a 35,000-word dispassionate analysis of how the war had occurred, and why it must now be won. His discursive tract covered a variety of subjects – historical, political, military, social – all driven by his desire to increase public understanding. As his biographer, St John Ervine, has observed, 'He was the sort of man that Jeremiah was, a man compelled to speak his mind when he felt that his people were erring.'[3] *Common Sense* sold 75,000 copies and provoked an uproar. Many people regarded Shaw as pro-German and a traitor, others shunned him, and the Dramatists' Club demanded his expulsion. Herbert Asquith said that Shaw ought to be shot; Sir John Squire that he ought to be tarred and feathered; and H.G. Wells that Shaw was 'like an idiot child screaming in a hospital.' A cartoon appeared of Shaw as a cross between an Irish terrier and a German dachshund decorated with an Iron Cross.[4] By war's end, however, many agreed that Shaw had been right and even prescient about some of the results. Even so, some people, like Jones, never overcame their enmity towards him.

Undeterred by the controversy, Shaw pressed on with his writing, working on such plays as *Heartbreak House* and *O'Flaherty, V.C.*, the latter revealing the common soldier's response to life and death in the trenches, and so-called heroism (pp. 27–30). In 1916 Shaw produced a supernatural fantasy short story, 'The Emperor and the Little Girl', in which Kaiser Wilhelm encounters a young girl on the battlefield in Belgium, and which captures the essence of the war's devastation (pp. 33–44). The story's simplicity and its haunting touches of realism expose the war's effect on those most vulnerable. Vulnerable too were conscientious objectors. Never a 'conchie' himself, Shaw nevertheless condemned the folly of removing conscientious objectors from worthwhile jobs (that had to be performed anyway) and imprisoning them. More than once Shaw was compelled to act on their behalf (pp. 30–2).

The war also affected Shaw directly: in 1916 a Zeppelin flew low over his house in Ayot St Lawrence and he explored its subsequent wreckage with almost ghoulish fascination (pp. 32–3). He found himself 'at the front' in 1917, the result of an invitation from Sir Douglas Haig so that Shaw could file suitable newspaper reports of his visit. There is almost a hint of enjoyment in Shaw's account (pp. 44–7) even after he and his party encountered an explosive too closely. Not so the news of friends' sons killed in action: his letter to Mrs Patrick Campbell on the death of her son in early 1918 resounds with Shaw's indignation (p. 47–8).

In the waning weeks of the war, Shaw produced *War Issues for Irishmen* (pp. 48–55), a pamphlet that argued for Irish participation on the British side (although the armistice signed on 11th November 1918 rendered the pamphlet moot). In it Shaw examined contemporary Irish politics, perhaps sometimes forgotten amidst the enormity of the Great War itself. For the Irish, nationalism and British rule were paramount concerns, and resulted in, for example, Sir Roger Casement's attempts to elicit German assistance against England in the Irish Nationalist cause, and in the Easter Rising of 1916, when 2,000 Irish Republicans fought to take control of Dublin. Neither endeavour was successful: Casement was hanged as a traitor, and fifteen of the Republican leaders were executed. Nevertheless, Shaw set forth vital arguments why Irishmen should enlist alongside the English.

'Peace is not only better than war, but infinitely more arduous,' was Shaw's sage observation in the Preface to *Heartbreak House* at the war's cessation. To promote an enduring peace settlement, in *Peace Conference Hints* (1919) Shaw urged the allies not to seek vengeful retribution on Germany, which would only sow the seeds for future discord – advice that was fatefully ignored. *Heartbreak House* finally emerged from its long gestation as Shaw's symbolic exploration of the era just passed, although the theatregoing public of 1921 was not in the mood for his Chekhovian masterwork. The play's published Preface rehearsed, more prosaically, the grim realities of the war and its futile sacrifices. He noted too how the public's reactions had been coloured by the ways in which different events in the war were reported and thus perceived (pp. 56–9). His 1924 Preface to *Saint Joan* (itself a debate about a charismatic leader and war) dissected further aspects of the war: military tribunals, so-called traitors, and the intolerance war breeds as insensate jingoism subjugates all to war. Such mindlessness was epitomised in the case of Edith Cavell, the English nurse executed in 1915 by the Germans for aiding sick soldiers to escape from Belgium to The Netherlands (pp. 59–61).

The First World War and its causes re-emerge in parts of *The Intelligent Woman's Guide to Socialism and Capitalism* (1928), a remarkable 200,000-word work that Ramsay MacDonald called the most important book after the Bible. Stimulated by a question from and dedicated to his sister-in-law (Mrs Mary Cholmondeley), the book is essentially a wide-ranging investigation of 'how wealth should be distributed in a respectable civilized country,' and is a distillation of Shaw's economic philosophy. Inevitably, the expansionist aspirations of early twentieth-century European countries figure in Shaw's analysis as he returns to demonstrating how war and capitalism are bound intimately together (pp.61–7).

Never far from controversy, Shaw again raised more than eyebrows in the 1920s and '30s with his admiration for dictators such as Mussolini, Stalin, and Hitler (he met personally with Stalin in 1931 in the company of Lord and Lady Astor). In response to criticism, Shaw defended his stance as pragmatic: 'It is equally irrelevant and silly to refuse to acknowledge the dictatorship of Il Duce because it was not achieved without all the usual villainies. The only question for us is whether he is doing his job well enough to induce the Italian nation to accept him *faute de mieux*. They do accept him, some of them *faute de mieux*, several of them with enthusiasm.'[5] Moreover, Shaw pointed out, Mussolini and Hitler had risen to power because they succeeded in stabilising their respective countries where democratic government had failed. Ironically, Hitler also owed his success to the terms of the Treaty of Versailles, which through harsh war reparations had brought Germany to its economic knees and thus opened the door for Hitler's rise. However, as the late eminent Shaw scholar Dan Laurence has noted, 'Shaw was unsympathetic to the concept of Aryan supremacy, and it was, finally, on the attendant issue of anti-Semitism that he was moved to draw the line, calling the Nazis' Judophobia "a very malignant disease," which "destroyed any credit the Nazis might have had."'[6] By 1938 Shaw's admiration had diminished considerably, and he lampooned Mussolini and Hitler as Bombardone and Battler in his successful play *Geneva*.

Shaw's friendship with Nancy, Lady Astor, and his involvement in her famous late-1930s 'Cliveden Set' (which Shaw regarded as a democratic talking shop) kept him in the forefront of political developments, and he again warned of impending war (pp.66–71). When the war came, one of Shaw's first protests was not political; instead, he objected to the mandatory closing of theatres and cinemas (pp.71–2). Potentially more controversial was his 'Uncommon Sense About the War,' a statement, albeit much terser, that echoed some of his 1914 assessments (pp.72–7). This time, however, his views did not arouse widespread animosity; indeed, the Foreign Secretary, Lord Halifax, supported publication of the article in order to sound out public sentiment. A planned 1940 broadcast (pp.77–81) fared less well, and was cancelled, Shaw thought, because Italy had just entered the war. However, Shaw's comments in it, including 'nine-tenths of what Mr Hitler says is true,' were probably considered too incendiary.

With the coming of the Blitz in 1940, Shaw and his wife Charlotte retired to life at their country home in Ayot St Lawrence, where life was less eventful than elsewhere (pp.81–2). Shaw joined others in calling for a ban on the bombing of cities by all combatants (pp.82–4), a plea that fell on deaf ears. One result was that Shaw suffered personally: 'My Whitehall flat has been blasted again, this time by a Robot. A window in my study was shivered into smithereens, my front door blown in.'[7]

Shaw (but not Charlotte) lived long enough to see the conclusion of the Second World War that simultaneously ushered in the atomic age and its horrendous possibilities (pp.84–5). The publication of *Geneva* provided Shaw with the recurrent opportunity for a retrospective on the war, and on Hitler in particular (pp.85–90), whilst the Nuremberg Military Tribunal sparked Shaw's novel remedy of circumventing the execution of convicted war criminals (p.90).

Even in his final years, Shaw remained occupied by the various facets of war, scrutinising both war's enduring futility and the possibility of hope for the future. The Young Man's behaviour in *Farfetched Fables* recalls both what the Devil had said about innate human characteristics and Undershaft's dedication to the armourer's creed (pp.90–3). However, Shaw could also predict that the destructive power of the atom might be turned to productive use: 'Atom disintegration will some day make heat cheaper than can coal-burning' ('Atomic Welfare', p.94). Such optimism, that society might benefit from the very means that could destroy it, is perhaps one reason for Shaw's thorough dissection of war throughout his lifetime: understanding the causes and effects of war is a crucial path to controlling it. Yet despite such optimism, were Shaw alive today, he might lament the events of the past half century or so and recall wryly the Sergeant's remark in *Too True to be Good* (1932): 'The great principle of soldiering, I take it, is that the world is kept going by the people who want the right thing killing the people who want the wrong thing. When the soldier is doing that, he is doing the work of God, which my mother brought me up to do.' And Shaw would agree once more with Hegel's adage: 'We learn from history that men never learn anything from history.'

– J.P. Wearing, 2009

Notes

1. 'Preface,' *Geneva* (New York, 1947), p.18.
2. G.K. Chesterton, *George Bernard Shaw* (New York, 1956), p.89.
3. St John Ervine, *Bernard Shaw: His Life, Work and Friends* (New York, 1956), p.463.
4. R.F. Rattray, *Bernard Shaw: A Chronicle* (New York, 1951), p.197.
5. *Collected Letters 1926–1950*, ed. Dan H. Laurence (London, 1988), p.44.
6. *Collected Letters 1926–1950*, p.457.
7. *Collected Letters 1926–1950*, p.716.

Note on the Text

The present selection of Shaw's writing on war draws from a much larger body of work, and includes the various literary forms he used to express his views. Shaw's somewhat eccentric but strongly held position on spelling and punctuation is retained in the extracts: for example, he uses 'shew', 'labor', 'dont', 'theyve', and '-ize' endings for verbs, instead of the standard 'show', 'labour', 'don't', 'they've', and '-ise'. However, in order to avoid confusion, he found himself obliged to use the normal 'I'll', 'it's', and 'he'll'. Except where otherwise stated, the dates given for plays refer to first performances.

I am grateful for the advice of Jeremy Crow of the Society of Authors, and Leonard Conolly, literary adviser to the Shaw Estate.

On War

Arms and the Man, Act I (1894)

'The Man' (Bluntschli), a Swiss mercenary fleeing Bulgarian soldiers, has taken refuge in Raina's bedroom. As they discuss the war, Bluntschli describes a cavalry charge led by Raina's fiancé, Sergius.

THE MAN Ive no ammunition. What use are cartridges in battle? I always carry chocolate instead; and I finished the last cake of that hours ago.

RAINA [*outraged in her most cherished ideals of manhood*] Chocolate! Do you stuff your pockets with sweets – like a schoolboy – even in the field?

THE MAN [*grinning*] Yes: isnt it contemptible? [*Hungrily*] I wish I had some now.

RAINA Allow me. [*She sails away scornfully to the chest of drawers, and returns with the box of confectionery in her hand*]. I am sorry I have eaten all except these. [*She offers him the box*].

THE MAN [*ravenously*] Youre an angel! [*He gobbles the contents*]. Creams! Delicious! [*He looks anxiously to see whether there are any more. There are none: he can only scrape the box with his fingers and suck them. When that nourishment is exhausted he accepts the inevitable with pathetic goodhumor, and says, with grateful emotion*] Bless you, dear lady! You can always tell an old soldier by the inside of his holsters and cartridge boxes. The young ones carry pistols and cartridges: the old ones, grub. Thank you. [*He hands back the box. She snatches it contemptuously from him and throws it away. He shies again, as if she had meant to strike him*]. Ugh! Dont do things so suddenly, gracious lady. Its mean to revenge yourself because I frightened you just now.

RAINA [*loftily*] Frighten *me*! Do you know, sir, that though I am only a woman, I think I am at heart as brave as you.

THE MAN I should think so. You havnt been under fire for three days as I have. I can stand two days without shewing it much; but no man can stand three days: I'm as nervous as a mouse.

3

[*He sits down on the ottoman, and takes his head in his hands*]. Would you like to see me cry?

RAINA [*alarmed*] No.

THE MAN If you would, all you have to do is to scold me just as if I were a little boy and you my nurse. If I were in camp now, theyd play all sorts of tricks on me.

RAINA [*a little moved*] I'm sorry. I wont scold you. [*Touched by the sympathy in her tone, he raises his head and looks gratefully at her: she immediately draws back and says stiffly*] You must excuse me: *our* soldiers are not like that. [*She moves away from the ottoman*].

THE MAN Oh yes they are. There are only two sorts of soldiers: old ones and young ones. Ive served fourteen years: half of your fellows never smelt powder before. Why, how is it that youve just beaten us? Sheer ignorance of the art of war, nothing else. [*Indignantly*] I never saw anything so unprofessional.

RAINA [*ironically*] Oh! was it unprofessional to beat you?

THE MAN Well, come! is it professional to throw a regiment of cavalry on a battery of machine guns, with the dead certainty that if the guns go off not a horse or man will ever get within fifty yards of the fire? I couldnt believe my eyes when I saw it.

RAINA [*eagerly turning to him, as all her enthusiasm and her dreams of glory rush back on her*] Did you see the great cavalry charge? Oh, tell me about it. Describe it to me.

THE MAN You never saw a cavalry charge, did you?

RAINA How could I?

THE MAN Ah, perhaps not. No: of course not! Well, it's a funny sight. It's like slinging a handful of peas against a window pane: first one comes; then two or three close behind him; and then all the rest in a lump.

RAINA [*her eyes dilating as she raises her clasped hands ecstatically*] Yes, first One! the bravest of the brave!

THE MAN [*prosaically*] Hm! you should see the poor devil pulling at his horse.

RAINA Why should he pull at his horse?

THE MAN [*impatient of so stupid a question*] It's running away with him, of course: do you suppose the fellow wants to get there before the others and be killed? Then they all come. You can tell the young ones by their wildness and their slashing. The old ones come bunched up under the number one guard: *they* know that theyre mere projectiles, and that it's no use trying to fight. The wounds are mostly broken knees, from the horses cannoning together.

RAINA Ugh! But I dont believe the first man is a coward. I know he is a hero!

THE MAN [*goodhumoredly*] Thats what youd have said if youd seen the first man in the charge today.

RAINA [*breathless, forgiving him everything*] Ah, I knew it! Tell me. Tell me about *him*.

THE MAN He did it like an operatic tenor. A regular handsome fellow, with flashing eyes and lovely moustache, shouting his war-cry and charging like Don Quixote at the windmills. We did laugh.

RAINA You dared to laugh!

THE MAN Yes; but when the sergeant ran up as white as a sheet, and told us theyd sent us the wrong ammunition, and that we couldnt fire a round for the next ten minutes, we laughed at the other side of our mouths. I never felt so sick in my life; though Ive been in one or two very tight places. And I hadnt even a revolver cartridge: only chocolate. We'd no bayonets: nothing. Of course, they just cut us to bits. And there was Don Quixote flourishing like a drum major, thinking he'd done the cleverest thing ever known, whereas he ought to be courtmartialled for it. Of all the fools ever let loose on a field of battle, that man must be the very maddest. He and his regiment simply committed suicide; only the pistol missed fire: thats all.

The Boer War (1899)

Shaw's letter to fellow Fabian George A.H. Samuel (b.1861) was written in about December 1899. As 'Marxian', Samuel wrote for various Labour journals.

You have to deal with a war declared by a peasant-proprietor State after laying in a careful supply of the best they can afford in the pencil bullet and explosive line. The Boer and the Britisher are both fighting animals, like all animals who live in a chronic panic of death and defeat. They are also carnivorous animals and alcohol-drinking animals. You know my sentiments on all three subjects. Do you expect me solemnly to inform a listening nation that the solution of the South African problem is that the lion shall lie down with the highly-armed lamb in mutual raptures of quakerism, vegetarianism, and teetotalism? No; hammer-headed as you are, you are not absurd enough for that. Now let us face the facts. Two hordes of predatory animals are fighting, after their manner, for the possession of South Africa, where neither of them has, or ever had, any business to be from the abstractly-moral, the virtuously indignant Radical, or (probably) the native point of view. Each of them, for party purposes, is trying to play-off this point of view against the other. 'Parricides; ye desert the flag of your country in its hour of extensive ripping and tearing by the Boer bullets,' cry the Conservatives. 'Jingo betrayers of the Prince of Peace,' cry the Liberals, 'ye are shedding the blood of a people rightly struggling to be free, and on the miserable pretext that it has declared war on ye.' Into the latter trap the Socialists [fall] by dozens, including Marxian who, from the bottom of the abyss, preaches at Shaw, who is smiling on the brink with the self-satisfaction of the fox who was too clever to be caught.

Now let me tell you some true things, Bishop Marxian. Number one: the moral position of the Boers and the British is precisely identical in every respect; that is, it does not exist. Two dogs are fighting for a bone thrown before them by Mrs Nature, an old-established butcher with a branch establishment in South Africa. The Socialist has only to consider which dog to back; that is, which dog will do most for Socialism if it wins.

Now – and here I am going to deliver a piece of exquisitely English wisdom – either the Boers will lick the British in this campaign, or the British will lick the Boers. You grant that, dont you? and admire its profundity.

Well, suppose the Boers beat the British. That takes South Africa out of our hands for ever as the United States were taken out. And what happens to South Africa? The Boers become a military power blazing with prestige, federate South Africa in a republic. If Rhodesia is recalcitrant or any colony loyal, 1861 will be repeated in a civil war to the death to consolidate Afrikanderdom.[1] You are still Marxian enough to know that in such a republic the dreams of Rhodes will be realized more thoroughly than Chamberlain and Downing Street could ever realize them.[2] All the throes of capitalism through which the United States have been dragged will be repeated as surely and as cruelly as if the martyrdoms of Lancashire and Pittsburgh had never been. This is what you are crying out for in the name of humanity, justice, Socialism, and all the other isms. As for me, if it is to be, it will be; but I am not enthusiastic.

The Boer War Revisited (1900)

Shaw's letter to Dr G.F. McCleary (1867–1962) was written on 24th May 1900. McCleary was Medical Officer of Health for Battersea and later worked for the Ministry of Health.

Furthermore I regard war as wasteful, demoralizing, un-necessary, and ludicrously and sordidly inglorious in its reality. This is my unconditional opinion. I *dont* mean war in a bad cause, or war against liberty, or war with any other qualification whatever: I mean war. I recognize no right of the good man to kill the bad man or to govern the bad man. The Boers have gone to war in defence of these rights. We have gone to war from pugnacity, greed and overfeeding. If the Boers had had any able statesmen, there would have been no war. If we had any statesmen, instead of the parcel of grown-up schoolboys of whom Milner[3] is a type, there would be no war. What of that? If the sky had fallen we should all have caught larks: that is all. If both parties regard the sword as the final arbiter, they must accept the consequences when the sword is drawn. If there were no such institution as war, no Socialist would be on the side of the Boers in this question any more than he would be on the side of Rhodes. I do not see then why we should take sides now that there is war. I am sorry they fight just as I am sorry they course hares and shoot pheasants and eat meat and believe in witch-inoculations as a charm against enteric fever. But why that should make me a pro-Boer when the Boer is just as bloodguilty as the Briton, and when I dont believe anything that the Boer believes, and dont believe that his pet institutions can ever produce anything but sordid misery for the mass of mankind, is a question which I leave you to answer. The fact is, every Englishman makes a fool of himself over this war on one side or the other. I, not being an Englishman, have kept my head; and there is the head and front of my offending.

Man and Superman, Act III, 'Don Juan in Hell' (1901)

The Devil discusses with Don Juan concepts of the 'Life Force' and the Nietzschean 'Superman'.

THE DEVIL And is Man any the less destroying himself for all this boasted brain of his? Have you walked up and down upon the earth lately? I have; and I have examined Man's wonderful inventions. And I tell you that in the arts of life man invents nothing; but in the arts of death he outdoes Nature herself, and produces by chemistry and machinery all the slaughter of plague, pestilence, and famine. The peasant I tempt today eats and drinks what was eaten and drunk by the peasants of ten thousand years ago; and the house he lives in has not altered as much in a thousand centuries as the fashion of a lady's bonnet in a score of weeks. But when he goes out to slay, he carries a marvel of mechanism that lets loose at the touch of his finger all the hidden molecular energies, and leaves the javelin, the arrow, the blowpipe of his father far behind. In the arts of peace Man is a bungler. I have seen his cotton factories and the like, with machinery that a greedy dog could have invented if it had wanted money instead of food. I know his clumsy typewriters and bungling loco-motives and tedious bicycles: they are toys compared to the Maxim gun,[4] the submarine torpedo boat. There is nothing in Man's industrial machinery but his greed and sloth: his heart is in his weapons. This marvellous force of Life of which you boast is a force of Death: Man measures his strength by his destructiveness. What is his religion? An excuse for hating me. What is his law? An excuse for hanging you. What is his morality? Gentility! an excuse for consuming without producing. What is his art? An excuse for gloating over pictures of slaughter. What are his politics? Either the worship of a despot because a despot can kill, or parlia-mentary cock-fighting. I spent an evening lately in a certain celebrated legislature, and heard a pot lecturing the kettle for its blackness, and ministers answering questions. When I left I chalked up on the door the old nursery saying 'Ask no questions and you will be told no lies'. I bought a sixpenny family magazine, and found it full of pictures of young men shooting and stabbing one another. I saw a man die: he was a London bricklayer's laborer with seven children. He left seventeen pounds club money; and his wife spent it all on his funeral and went into the workhouse with the children next day. She would not have spent sevenpence on her children's schooling: the law had to force her to let them be taught gratuitously; but on death she spent all she had. Their imagination glows, their energies rise up at the idea of death, these people: they love it; and the more horrible it is the more they enjoy it.

Major Barbara, Act III (1905)

After visiting a Salvation Army shelter in Act II, Undershaft shows off his model armaments factory with its ideal working conditions to his family and to Cusins, potentially his successor. Undershaft explains the armourer's creed.

UNDERSHAFT [*with a touch of brutality*] The government of your country! *I* am the government of your country: I, and Lazarus. Do you suppose that you and half a dozen amateurs like you, sitting in a row in that foolish gabble shop, can govern Undershaft and Lazarus? No, my friend: you will do what pays *us*. You will make war when it suits us, and keep peace when it doesnt. You will find out that trade requires certain measures when we have decided on those measures. When I want anything to keep my dividends up, you will discover that my want is a national need. When other people want something to keep my dividends down, you will call out the police and military. And in return you shall have the support and applause of my newspapers, and the delight of imagining that you are a great statesman. Government of your country! Be off with you, my boy, and play with your caucuses and leading articles and historic parties and great leaders and burning questions and the rest of your toys. I am going back to my counting-house to pay the piper and call the tune.

* * *

BARBARA Is the bargain closed, Dolly? Does your soul belong to him now?

CUSINS No: the price is settled: that is all. The real tug of war is still to come. What about the moral question?

LADY BRITOMART There is no moral question in the matter at all, Adolphus. You must simply sell cannons and weapons to people whose cause is right and just, and refuse them to foreigners and criminals.

UNDERSHAFT [*determinedly*] No: none of that. You must keep the true faith of an Armorer, or you dont come in here.

CUSINS What on earth is the true faith of an Armorer?

UNDERSHAFT To give arms to all men who offer an honest price for them, without respect of persons or principles: to aristocrat and republican, to Nihilist and Tsar, to Capitalist and Socialist, to Protestant and Catholic, to burglar and policeman, to black man, white man and yellow man, to all sorts and conditions, all nationalities, all faiths, all follies, all causes and all crimes. The first Undershaft wrote up in his shop IF GOD GAVE THE HAND, LET NOT MAN WITHHOLD THE SWORD. The second wrote up ALL HAVE THE RIGHT TO FIGHT: NONE HAVE THE RIGHT TO JUDGE. The third wrote up TO MAN THE WEAPON: TO HEAVEN THE VICTORY. The fourth had no literary turn; so he did not write up anything; but he sold cannons to Napoleon under the nose of George the Third. The fifth wrote up PEACE SHALL NOT PREVAIL SAVE WITH A SWORD IN HER HAND. The sixth, my master, was the best of all. He wrote up NOTHING IS EVER DONE IN THIS WORLD UNTIL MEN ARE PREPARED TO KILL ONE ANOTHER IF IT IS NOT DONE. After that, there was nothing left for the seventh to say. So he wrote up, simply, UNASHAMED.

CUSINS My good Machiavelli, I shall certainly write something up on the wall; only, as I shall write it in Greek, you wont be able to read it. But as to your Armorer's faith, if I take my neck out of the noose of my own morality I am not going to put it into the noose of yours. I shall sell cannons to whom I please and refuse them to whom I please. So there!

UNDERSHAFT From the moment when you become Andrew Undershaft, you will never do as you please again. Dont come here lusting for power, young man.

CUSINS If power were my aim I should not come here for it. You have no power.

UNDERSHAFT None of my own, certainly.

CUSINS I have more power than you, more will. You do not drive this place: it drives you. And what drives the place?

UNDERSHAFT [*enigmatically*] A will of which I am a part.

BARBARA [*startled*] Father! Do you know what you are saying; or are you laying a snare for my soul?

CUSINS Dont listen to his metaphysics, Barbara. The place is driven by the most rascally part of society, the money hunters, the pleasure hunters, the military promotion hunters; and he is their slave.

UNDERSHAFT Not necessarily. Remember the Armorer's Faith. I will take an order from a good man as cheerfully as from a bad one. If you good people prefer preaching and shirking to buying my weapons and fighting the rascals, dont blame me. I can make cannons: I cannot make courage and conviction.

'Armaments and Conscription: A Triple Alliance against War' (1913)

Shaw's proposal was published in The Daily Chronicle, *18th March 1913.*

Our first step, therefore, should be to propose to France and Germany a triple alliance, the terms being that if France attack Germany we combine with Germany to crush France, and if Germany attack France, we combine with France to crush Germany. Germany doubts whether France would come into this alliance in her present temper; but I really do not see how she could help it if Germany consented, because we should conclude a dual alliance if we could not have a triple one, in which case France would be in the position that whereas she could not attack Germany without fighting us at the same time, Germany could attack her without our interference. The alliance would guarantee, further, that if any other Power were to attack either France or Germany, the three would line up together against that Power. From that starting-point we might enlarge the combination by accessions from Holland and the Scandinavian kingdoms and finally achieve the next step in civilization, the policing of Europe against war and the barbarians… If we cannot have an effective army for all purposes, we may as well shut up shop as far as foreign policy is concerned until we make an end of war; and that we can only do so by being prepared to make war on war… As a Socialist I am very strongly in favour of compulsory service. All income tax returns and insurance cards should in future have a column for chest measurements and age; and all able-bodied persons should be obliged to give the country 35 years' service, of which a few would be devoted to military training.

Common Sense About the War (1914)

Published in The New Statesman, *14th November 1914, as a supplement. As part of the background to his tract, Shaw castigated the Foreign Secretary, Sir Edward Grey (1862–1933), for conducting secret diplomacy that failed to make clear Britain's intentions if Germany violated Belgian neutrality, and for then using the violation as a pretext for declaring war. Shaw also equated the German military Junker class with British country squires and militarists, all of whom were itching for the opportunity to fight. What follow are some of Shaw's salient points.*

I see both nations [Britain and Germany] duped, but alas! not quite unwillingly duped, by their Junkers and Militarists into wreaking on one another the wrath they should have spent in destroying Junkerism and Militarism in their own country. And I see the Junkers and Militarists of England and Germany jumping at the chance they have longed for in vain for many years of smashing one another and establishing their own oligarchy as the dominant military power in the world. No doubt the heroic remedy for this tragic misunderstanding is that both armies should shoot their officers and go home to gather in their harvests in the villages and make a revolution in the towns; and though this is not at present a practicable solution, it must be frankly mentioned, because it or something like it is always a possibility in a defeated conscript army if its commanders push it beyond human endurance when its eyes are opening to the fact that in murdering its neighbors it is biting off its nose to vex its face, besides riveting the intolerable yoke of Militarism and Junkerism more tightly than ever on its own neck. But there is no chance – or, as our Junkers would put it, no danger – of our soldiers yielding to such an ecstasy of common sense. They have enlisted voluntarily; they are not defeated nor likely to be; their communications are intact and their meals reasonably punctual; they are as pugnacious as their officers; and in fighting Prussia they are fighting a more deliberate, conscious, tyrannical, per- sonally insolent, and dangerous Militarism than their own. Still, even for a voluntary professional army, that possibility exists, just as for the civilian there is a limit beyond which taxation, bankruptcy, privation, terror, and inconvenience cannot be pushed without revolution or a social dissolution more ruinous than submission to conquest.

'Six of One: Half-a-Dozen of the Other'
I myself steadily advocated the formation of a formidable armament, and ridiculed the notion that we, who are wasting hundreds of millions annually on idlers and wasters, could not

easily afford double, treble, quadruple our military and naval expenditure. I advocated the compulsion of every man to serve his country, both in war and peace. The idlers and wasters, perceiving dimly that I meant the cost to come out of their pockets, and meant to use the admission that riches should not exempt a man from military service as an illustration of how absurd it is to allow them to exempt him from civil service, did not embrace my advocacy with enthusiasm; so I must reaffirm it now lest it should be supposed that I am condemning those whose proceedings I am describing. Though often horribly wrong in principle, they were quite right in practice as far as they went. But they must stand to their guns now that the guns are going off. They must not pretend that they were harmless Radical lovers of peace, and that the propaganda of Militarism and of inevitable war between England and Germany is a Prussian infamy for which the Kaiser[5] must be severely punished. That is not fair, not true, not gentlemanly. We began it; and if they met us half-way, as they certainly did, it is not for us to reproach them. When the German fire-eaters drank to The Day (of Armageddon) they were drinking to the day of which our Navy League fire-eaters had first said, 'It's bound to come.' Therefore let us have no more nonsense about the Prussian Wolf and the British Lamb, the Prussian Machiavelli and the English Evangelist. We cannot shout for years that we are boys of the bulldog breed, and then suddenly pose as gazelles. No. When Europe and America come to settle the treaty that will end this business (for America is concerned in it as much as we are) they will not deal with us as the lovable and innocent victims of a treacherous tyrant and a savage soldiery. They will have to consider how these two incorrigibly pugnacious and inveterately snobbish peoples who have snarled at one another for forty years with bristling hair and grinning fangs, and are now rolling over with their teeth in one another's throats, are to be tamed into trusty watchdogs of the peace of the world.

'Learning Nothing: Forgetting Everything'

Militarism must be classed as one of the most inconsiderately foolish of the bogus 'sciences' which the last half century has produced in such profusion, and which have the common characteristic of revolting all sane souls, and being stared out of countenance by the broad facts of human experience. The only rule of thumb that can be hazarded on the strength of actual practice is that wars to maintain or upset the Balance of Power between States, called by inaccurate people Balance of Power wars, and by accurate people Jealousy of Power wars, never establish the desired peaceful and secure equilibrium. They may exercise pugnacity, gratify spite, assuage a wound to national pride, or enhance or dim a military reputation; but that is all. And the reason is, as I shall shew very conclusively later on, that there is only one way in which one nation can really disable another, and that is a way which no civilized nation dare even discuss.

'Recruiting'

We must have the best army in Europe; and we shall not get it under existing arrangements. We are passing out of the first phase of the war fever, in which men flock to the colours by instinct, by romantic desire for adventure, by the determination not, as Wagner put it, 'to let their lives be governed by fear of the end',[6] by simple destitution through unemployment, by rancor and pugnacity excited by the inventions of the Press, by a sense of duty inculcated in platform orations which would not stand half an hour's discussion, by the incitements and taunts of elderly non-combatants and maidens with a taste for mischief, and by the verses of poets jumping at the cheapest chance in their underpaid profession. The difficulty begins when all the men susceptible to these inducements are enlisted, and we have to draw on the solid, sceptical, sensible residuum who know the value of their lives and services and liberties, and will not give them except on substantial and honorable conditions. These Ironsides know that it is one thing to fight for your country, and quite another to let your wife and children starve to save our rich idlers from a rise in the Supertax. They also know that it is one thing to wipe out the Prussian drill sergeant and snob officer as the enemies of manhood and honor, and another to let that sacred mission be made an excuse for subjecting us to exactly the same tyranny in England. They have not forgotten the 'On the knee' episode, nor the floggings in our military prisons, nor the scandalous imprisonment of Tom Mann, nor the warnings as to military law and barrack life contained even in Robert Blatchford's testimony that the army made a man of him.[7]

'What the Labor Party Owes to the Army'
And here is where the Labor Party should come in. The Labor Party's business is to abolish the Militarist soldier, who is only a quaint survival of the King's footman (himself a still quainter survival of the medieval baron's retainer), and substitute for him a trained combatant with full civil rights, receiving the Trade Union rate of wages proper to a skilled worker at a dangerous trade. It must co-operate with the Trade Unions in fixing this moral minimum wage for the citizen soldier, and in obtaining for him a guarantee that the wage shall continue until he obtains civil employment on standard terms at the conclusion of the war. It must make impossible the scandal of a monstrously rich peer (his riches, the automatic result of ground landlordism, having 'no damned nonsense of merit about them') proclaiming the official weekly allowance for the child of the British soldier in the trenches. That allowance is eighteenpence, being less than one third of the standard allowance for an illegitimate child under an affiliation order. And the Labor Party must deprive the German bullet of its present double effect in killing an Englishman in France and simultaneously reducing his widow's subsistence to seven-and-sixpence a week. Until this is done, we are simply provoking Providence to destroy us.

I wish I could say that it is hardly necessary to add that Trade Unionism must be instituted in the Army, so that there shall be accredited secretaries in the field to act as a competent medium of communication between the men on service and the political representatives of their class at the War Office (for I shall propose this representative innovation presently). It will shock our colonels; but I know of no bodies of men for whom repeated and violent shocking is more needed and more likely to prove salutary than the regimental messes of the British army. One rather pleasant shock in store for them is the discovery that an officer and a gentleman, whose sole professional interest is the honor and welfare of his country, and who is bound to the mystical equality of life-and-death duty for all alike, will get on much more easily with a Trade Union secretary than a commercial employer whose aim is simply private profit and who regards every penny added to the wages of his employees as a penny taken off his own income. Howbeit, whether the colonels like it or not – that is, whether they have become accustomed to it or not – it has to come, and its protection from Junker prejudice is another duty of the Labor Party. The Party as a purely political body must demand that the defender of his country shall retain his full civil rights unimpaired; that the unnecessary, mischievous, dishonorable and tyrannical slave code called military law, which at its most savagely stern point produced only Wellington's complaint that 'it is impossible to get a command obeyed in the British Army,' be carted away to the rubbish heap of exploded superstitions; and that if Englishmen are not to be allowed to serve their country in the field as freely as they do in the numerous civil industries in which neglect and indiscipline are as dangerous as they are in war, their leaders and Parliamentary representatives will not recommend them to serve at all. In wartime these things may not matter: discipline either goes by the board or keeps itself under the pressure of the enemy's cannon; and bullying sergeants and insolent officers have something else to do than to provoke men they dislike into striking them and then reporting them for two years hard labor without trial by jury. In battle such officers are between two fires. But soldiers are not always, or even often, at war; and the dishonor of abdicating dearly-bought rights and liberties is a stain both on war and peace. Now is the time to get rid of that stain. If any officer cannot command men without it, as civilians and police inspectors do, that officer has mistaken his profession and had better come home.

'Obsolete Tests in the Army'
The Labor Party should also set its face firmly against the abandonment of Red Cross work and finance, or the support of soldiers' families, or the patrolling of the streets, to amateurs who regard the war as a wholesome patriotic exercise, or as the latest amusement in the way of charity bazaars, or as a fountain of self-righteousness. Civil volunteering is needed urgently enough: one of the difficulties of war is that it creates in certain departments a demand so abnormal that no peace establishment can cope with it. But the volunteers should be disciplined and paid: we are not so poor that we need sponge on anyone. And in hospital and medical service war ought not at present to cost more than peace would if the victims of our commercial system were properly tended, and our Public Health service adequately extended and manned. We should therefore treat our Red Cross department as if it were destined to become a permanent service. No charity and no amateur anarchy and incompetence should be tolerated. As to allowing that admirable detective agency for the defence of the West End against begging letter writers, the Charity Organization Society, to touch the soldier's home, the very suggestion is an outrage.[8] The C.O.S., the Poor Law, and the charitable amateur, whether of the patronizing or prying or gushing variety, must be kept as far from the army and its folk as if they were German spies. The business of our fashionable amateurs is to pay Income Tax and Supertax. This time they will have to pay through the nose, vigorously wrung for that purpose by the House of Commons; so they had better set their own houses in order and leave the business of the war to be officially and responsibly dealt with and paid for at full standard rates.

'The War Office Bait of Starvation'
[The War Office] suddenly began to placard the country with frantic assurances to its five-thousand-a-year friends that they would be 'discharged with all possible speed THE MINUTE THE WAR IS OVER.' Only considerations of space restrained them, I presume, from adding 'LAWN TENNIS, SHOOTING, AND ALL THE DELIGHTS OF FASHIONABLE LIFE CAN BE RESUMED IMMEDIATELY ON THE fiRING OF THE LAST SHOT.' Now what does this mean to the wage worker? Simply that the moment he is no longer wanted in the trenches he will be flung back into the labor market to sink or swim without an hour's respite. If we had had a Labor representative or two to help in drawing up these silly placards – I am almost tempted to say if we had had any human being of any class with half the brains of a rabbit there – the placards would have contained a solemn promise that no single man should be discharged at the conclusion of the war, save at his own request, until a job had been found for him in civil life. I ask the heavens, with a shudder, do these class-blinded people in authority really intend to take a million men out of their employment; turn them into soldiers; and then at one blow hurl them back, utterly unprovided for, into the streets?

'Delusive Promises'
The middle and upper classes are nearly as bad as the War Office. They talk of keeping every man's place open for him until the end of the war. Obviously this is flatly impossible. Some places can be kept, and no doubt are being kept. Some functions are suspended by the war and cannot be resumed until the troops return to civil life and resume them. Employers are so hardened to the daily commercial necessity for discharging men without a thought as to what is to become of them that they are quite ready to undertake to sack the replacers when the troops come back. Also the return of peace may be followed by a revival of trade in which employment may not be hard to find, even by discharged soldiers, who are always passed over in the

labor market in favor of civilians, as those well know who have the task of trying to find places for them. But these considerations do not justify an attempt to persuade recruits that they can go off soldiering for months – they are told by Lord Kitchener that it will probably be for years[9] – and then come back and walk to their benches or into their offices and pick up their work as if they had left only the night before. The very people who are promising this are raising the cry 'business as usual' in the same breath. How can business be carried on as usual, or carried on at all, on unoccupied office stools and at counters with no men behind them? Such rubbish is an insult to the recruit's intelligence. These promises of keeping places open were made to the men who enlisted for South Africa, and were of course broken, as a promise to supply green cheese by quarrying the moon would have been broken. New employees must be found to do the work of the men who are in the field; and these new ones will not all be thrown into the street when the war is over to make room for discharged soldiers, even if a good many of these soldiers are not disqualified by their new training and habits for their old employment. I repeat, there is only one assurance that can be given to the recruits without grossly and transparently deluding them; and that is that they shall not be discharged, except at their own request, until civil employment is available for them.

'Funking Controversy'

But it is now proposed to suspend all popular liberties and constitutional safeguards: to muzzle the Press, and actually to have no contests at bye-elections! This is more than a little too much. We have submitted to have our letters, our telegrams, our newspapers censored, our dividends delayed, our trains cut off, our horses and even our houses commandeered, our streets darkened, our restaurants closed, and ourselves shot dead on the public highways when we were slow to realize that some excited person bawling in the distance was a sentry challenging us. But that we are to be politically gagged and enslaved as well; that the able-bodied soldier in the trenches, who depends on the able-minded civilian at home to guard the liberties of his country and protect him from carelessness or abuse of power by the authorities whom he must blindly and dumbly obey, is to be betrayed the moment his back is turned to his fellow citizens and his face to the foe, is not patriotism: it is the paralysis of mortal funk: it is the worst kind of cowardice in the face of the enemy. Let us hear no more of it, but contest our elections like men, and regain the ancient political prestige of England at home as our expeditionary force has regained it abroad.

'Natural Limits to the Duration of the War'

Now for the terms of peace. It is time to take that subject in hand; for Lord Kitchener's notion that we are going to settle down to years of war as we did a century ago is soldierly, but not sensible. It is, of course, physically possible for us to continue for twenty years digging trenches and shelling German troops and shoving German armies back when they are not shoving us, whilst old women pull turnips and tend goats in the fire zones across which soldiers run to shelter. But we cannot afford to withdraw a million male adults who have passed a strictish health test from the work of parentage for several years unless we intend to breed our next generation from parents with short sight, varicose veins, rotten teeth, and deranged internal organs. Soldiers do not think of these things: 'theirs not to reason why: theirs but to do and die'; but sensible civilians have to. And even soldiers know that you cannot make ammunition as fast as you can burn it, nor produce men and horses as instantaneously as you can kill them by machinery. It would be well, indeed, if our papers, instead of writing of ten-inch shells, would speak of £1,000 shells, and regimental bands occasionally finish the National Anthem and the Brabançonne and the Marseillaise with the old strain, 'That's the way the money goes: Pop goes the Ten Inch.'[10]

'The Commercial Attitude'

First, our commercial main body, which thinks that chivalry is not business, and that rancor is childish, but cannot see why we should not make the Germans pay damages and supply us with some capital to set the City going again, forgetting that when France did that after 1871 for Berlin,[11] Berlin was set going so effectually that it went headlong to a colossal financial smash, whilst the French peasant who had provided the capital from his old stocking throve soberly on the interest at the expense of less vital classes. Unfortunately Germany has set the example of this kind of looting.

'Vindictive Damages'

And we must not let ourselves be tempted to soil our hands under pretext of vindictive damages. The man who thinks that all the money in Germany could pay for the life of a single British drummer boy ought to be shot merely as an expression of the feeling that he is unfit to live. We stake our blood as the Germans stake theirs; and in that *ganz besonderes Saft*[12] alone should we pay or accept payment. We had better not say to the Kaiser at the end of the war, 'Scoundrel: you can never replace the Louvain library, nor the sculpture of Rheims; and it follows logically that you shall empty your pockets into ours.' Much better say: 'God forgive us all!' If we cannot rise to this, and must soil our hands with plunder, at least let us call it plunder, and not profane our language and our souls by giving it fine names.

'Our Annihilationists'

Then we shall have the Militarists, who will want to have Germany 'bled white', dismembered, broken, starved, so that she may never do it again. Well, that is quite simple, if you are Militarist enough to do it. Loading Germany with debt will not do it. Towing her fleet into Portsmouth or sinking it will not do it. Annexing provinces and colonies will not do it. The effective method is far shorter and more practical. What has made

Germany formidable in this war? Obviously her overwhelmingly superior numbers.

'Why Not Kill the German Women?'

Well, there is no obscurity about that problem. Those Germans who took but an instant to kill had taken the travail of a woman for three-quarters of a year to breed, and eighteen years to ripen for the slaughter. All we have to do is to kill, say, 75 per cent of all the women in Germany under sixty. Then we may leave Germany her fleet and her money, and say, 'Much good may they do you!' Why not, if you are really going in to be what you, never having read 'this Neech they talk of', call a Nietzschean Superman?[13] War is not an affair of sentiment. Some of our newspapers complain that the Germans kill the wounded and fire on field hospitals and Red Cross Ambulances. These same newspapers fill their columns with exultant accounts of how our wounded think nothing of modern bullet wounds and hope to be back at the front in a week, which I take to be the most direct incitement to the Germans to kill the wounded that could be devised. It is no use being virtuously indignant: 'stone dead hath no fellow' is an English proverb, not a German one. Even the killing of prisoners is an Agincourt tradition.[14] Now it is not more cowardly to kill a woman than to kill a wounded man. And there is only one reason why it is a greater crime to kill a woman than a man, and why women have to be spared and protected when men are exposed and sacrificed. That reason is that the destruction of the women is the destruction of the community. Men are comparatively of no account: kill 90 per cent of the German men, and the remaining 10 per cent can repeople her. But kill the women, and *Delenda est Carthago*.[15]

'The Sensible People'

Finally we come to the only body of opinion in which there is any hope for civilization: the opinion of the people who are bent, not on gallantry nor revenge nor plunder nor pride nor panic nor glory nor any of the invidiousnesses of patriotism, but on the problem of how to so redraw the map of Europe and reform its political constitutions that this abominable crime and atrocious nuisance, a European war, shall not easily occur again. The map is very important; for the open sores which have at last suppurated and burst after having made the world uneasy for years, were produced by altering the color of Alsace and Lorraine and of Bosnia and Herzegovina on the map. And the new map must be settled, not by conquest, but by consent of the people immediately concerned. One of the broken treaties of Europe which has been mentioned less frequently of late than the Belgian treaty is the treaty of Prague, by which a plebiscite was to have been taken on the subject of the nationality of Schleswig and Holstein.[16] That plebiscite has never been taken. It may have to be taken, with other plebiscites, before this war is settled.

'The Russian Russians and Their Prussian Tsars'
But it cannot be too frankly said at the outset that any attempt to settle Europe on the basis of the present hemming in of a consolidated Germany and German Austria by a hostile combination of Russia and the extreme western States against it, would go to pieces by its own inherent absurdity, just as it has already exploded most destructively by its own instability. Until Russia becomes a federation of several separate democratic States, and the Tsar is either promoted to the honorable position of hereditary President or else totally abolished, the eastern boundary of the League of Peace must be the eastern boundary of Swedish, German and Italian civilization; and Poland must stand between it and the quite different, and for the moment unassimilable, civilization of Russia, whose friendship we could not really keep on any other terms.

'The Disarmament Delusion'
The League of Peace must have a first-rate armament, or the League of War will very soon make mincemeat of it. The notion

that the men of evil intent are to have all the weapons will not work. Theoretically, all our armaments should be pooled. But as we, the British Empire, will most certainly not pool our defences with anyone, and as we have not the very smallest intention of disarming, and will go on building gun for gun and ship for ship in step with even our dearest friends if we see the least risk of our being left in a position of inferiority, we cannot with any countenance demand that other Powers shall do what we will not do ourselves. Our business is not to disable ourselves or anyone else, but to organize a balance of military power against war, whether made by ourselves or any other Power; and this can be done only by a combination of armed and fanatical Pacifists of all nations, not by a crowd of non-combatants wielding deprecations, remonstrances, and Christmas cards.

'America's Example: War at a Year's Notice'
I conclude that we might all very well make a beginning by pledging ourselves as America has done to The Hague tribunal not to take up arms in any cause that has been less than a year under arbitration, and to treat any western Power refusing this pledge as an unpopular and suspicious member of the European club. To break such a pledge would be an act of brigandage; and the need for suppressing brigandage cannot be regarded as an open question.

'The Only Real World Danger'
The one danger before us that nothing can avert but a general raising of human character through the deliberate cultivation and endowment of democratic virtue without consideration of property and class, is the danger created by inventing weapons capable of destroying civilization faster than we produce men who can be trusted to use them wisely. At present we are handling them like children. Now children are very pretty, very lovable, very affectionate creatures (sometimes); and a child can make nitro-glycerine or chloride of nitrogen as well as a man

if it is taught to do so. We have sense enough not to teach it; but we do teach the grown-up children. We actually accompany that dangerous technical training with solemn moral lessons in which the most destructive use of these forces at the command of kings and capitalists is inculcated as heroism, patriotism, glory and all the rest of it. It is all very well to fire cannons at the Kaiser for doing this; but we do it ourselves. It is therefore undeniably possible that a diabolical rhythm may be set up in which civilization will rise periodically to the point at which explosives powerful enough to destroy it are discovered, and will then be shattered and thrown back to a fresh start with a few starving and ruined survivors. H.G. Wells and Anatole France have prefigured that result in fiction;[17] and I cannot deny the strength of its probability; for if England and Germany can find no better way of celebrating their arrival at the highest point of civilization yet attained than setting out to blow one another to fragments with fulminates, it would seem that the peace of the neutral States is the result, not of their being more civilized, but less heavily armed.

O'Flaherty, V.C.: A Recruiting Pamphlet (1915)

A planned 1915 performance of the play in Dublin was cancelled by the authorities; the first performance was at the Belgian front in 1917. As a holder of the Victoria Cross, O'Flaherty has been enlisted to assist General Sir Pearce Madigan's recruiting campaign in O'Flaherty's village in Ireland.

SIR PEARCE Why cant you explain to her [O'Flaherty's mother] what the war is about?

O'FLAHERTY Arra, sir, how the divil do I know what the war is about?

SIR PEARCE [*rising again and standing over him*] What! O'Flaherty: do you know what you are saying? You sit there wearing the Victoria Cross for having killed God knows how many Germans; and you tell me you dont know why you did it!

O'FLAHERTY Asking your pardon, Sir Pearce. I tell you no such thing. I know quite well why I kilt them. I kilt them because I was afeard that, if I didnt, theyd kill me.

SIR PEARCE [*giving it up and sitting down again*] Yes, yes, of course; but have you no knowledge of the causes of the war? of the interests at stake? of the importance – I may almost say – in fact I will say – the sacred rights for which we are fighting? Dont you read the papers?

O'FLAHERTY I do when I can get them. Theres not many newsboys crying the evening paper in the trenches. They do say, Sir Pearce, that we shall never beat the Boshes until we make Horatio Bottomley[18] Lord Leftnant of England. Do you think thats true, sir?

SIR PEARCE Rubbish, man! theres no Lord Lieutenant in England: the king is Lord Lieutenant. It's a simple question of patriotism. Does patriotism mean nothing to you?

O'FLAHERTY It means different to me than what it would to you, sir. It means England and England's king to you. To me and the like of me, it means talking about the English just the way the English papers talk about the Boshes. And what good has it ever done here in Ireland? It's kept me ignorant because it filled up my mother's mind, and she thought it ought to fill up mine too. It's kept Ireland poor, because instead of trying to better ourselves we thought we was the fine fellows of patriots when we were speaking evil of Englishmen that was as poor as ourselves and maybe as good as ourselves. The Boshes I kilt was more knowledgable men than me: and what better am I now that Ive kilt them? What better is anybody?

SIR PEARCE [*huffed, turning a cold shoulder to him*] I am sorry the terrible experience of this war – the greatest war ever fought – has taught you no better, O'Flaherty.

O'FLAHERTY [*preserving his dignity*] I dont know about it's being a great war, sir. It's a big war; but thats not the same thing.

Father Quinlan's new church is a big church: you might take the little old chapel out of the middle of it and not miss it. But my mother says there was more true religion in the old chapel. And the war has taught me that may be she was right.

SIR PEARCE [*grunts sulkily*]!!

O'FLAHERTY [*respectfully but doggedly*] And theres another thing it's taught me too, sir, that concerns you and me, if I may make bold to tell it to you.

SIR PEARCE [*still sulkily*] I hope it's nothing you oughtnt to say to me, O'Flaherty.

O'FLAHERTY It's this, sir: that I'm able to sit here now and talk to you without humbugging you; and thats what not one of your tenants or your tenants' childer ever did to you before in all your long life. It's a true respect I'm shewing you at last, sir. Maybe youd rather have me humbug you and tell you lies as I used, just as the boys here, God help them, would rather have me tell them how I fought the Kaiser, that all the world knows I never saw in my life, than tell them the truth. But I cant take advantage of you the way I used, not even if I seem to be wanting in respect to you and cocked up by winning the Cross.

SIR PEARCE [*touched*] Not at all, O'Flaherty. Not at all.

O'FLAHERTY Sure whats the Cross to me, barring the little pension it carries? Do you think I dont know that theres hundreds of men as brave as me that never had the luck to get anything for their bravery but a curse from the sergeant, and the blame for the faults of them that ought to have been their betters? Ive learnt more than youd think, sir; for how would a gentleman like you know what a poor ignorant conceited creature I was when I went from here into the wide world as a soldier? What use is all the lying, and pretending, and humbugging, and letting on, when the day comes to you that your comrade is killed in the trench beside you, and you dont as much as look round at him until you trip over his poor body, and then all you say is to ask why the hell the stretcher-bearers dont take it out of the way. Why should I read the papers to be humbugged and lied to by them that had the cunning to stay at home and send me to fight for them? Dont talk to me or to any soldier of the war being right. No war is right; and all the holy water that Father Quinlan ever blessed couldnt make one right. There, sir! Now you know what O'Flaherty V.C. thinks; and youre wiser so than the others that only knows what he done.

SIR PEARCE [*making the best of it, and turning goodhumoredly to him again*] Well, what you did was brave and manly, anyhow.

O'FLAHERTY God knows whether it was or not, better than you nor me, General. I hope He wont be too hard on me for it, anyhow.

'Conscientious Objectors' (1915)

Shaw's letter to the editor of The Nation *was published 27th May 1915. Eric B.W. Chappelow (1890–1957) was also a poet; a later court martial of him was reported in* The Times, *21st April 1916. Shaw wrote several similar letters including one on behalf of the composer, Rutland Boughton (1878–1960).*

The case of Mr Chappelow is much more important than it appears in the statement made by himself and circulated by his friends... Mr Chappelow not only took all possible steps to obtain exemption as a conscientious objector under the Act, but actually obtained it. Then, if you please, the military authority reclaimed him on the ground that if he would not fight, some use or other could be made of him in barracks, as he was an able-bodied young man in his twenties who was doing nothing for his country. And it was on this plea that he was recaptured.

Now some readers will say that the military authority was quite right. Apparently, the tribunal thought so. Let us see. Mr Chappelow was employed in the Education Department of the London County Council. The decision therefore meant that public education is of no service to the country; and that to take an educated man of special literary talent and aptitude from the work of national education, and to set him to sweep barracks, dig latrines, or wait at table on an officers' mess is to effect a stroke of national economy which will materially help to win the war. The ignorant folly of such a conclusion would be disheartening enough even if Mr Chappelow were now actually sweeping the barracks or digging the latrines, which are quite honorable occupations, though no sane civil authority, nor even a military one not exceptionally stupid, would dream of wasting skilled intellectual workers on them. But Mr Chappelow is neither sweeping or digging. He is not only eating his head off in prison, but holding up the labor and energy of other men guarding him, feeding him, book-keeping and reporting about him, and talking and writing a great deal of nonsense concerning his case. In view of so idiotic a result, I can only say that if the military authority is proud of itself, and feels that the Germans are reeling under the effects of its activity, its facility in self-satisfaction is to be envied.

If I were President of the Board of Education, and any military authority alive took a member of the national staff of education from his work and thrust him into a barrack on the ground that anything he could be set to do there was more important than education, I would have my man out with an abject apology, and that military authority lectured severely on the need for a little common sense, before the end of the week. I naturally expected our Minister[19] to do something of the sort when the facts were placed before him. But he still has the fatal modesty of a Labor member who has not yet acquired the regular governing class touchiness on the departmental point of honor. He took it lying down; and, as far as he is concerned, Mr Chappelow may do his six months waste of the national resources unhindered. Indeed, he may spend the rest of his life in prison; for I presume that at the expiration of his sentence he will be returned to barracks, will again refuse to serve, will again be court–martialled, and again sent back to be a burden on the British taxpayer and a drain on British military energy, when he might be doing his work in the education department if people only had twopennorth of sense.

Shaw and a Zeppelin (1916)

Shaw's letter to his friends and fellow Fabians, Beatrice (1858–1943) and Sidney (1859–1947) Webb, was written 5th October 1916.

The Potters Bar Zeppelin manoeuvred over the Welwyn valley for about half an hour before it came round and passed London-wards with the nicest precision over our house straight along our ridge tiles. It made a magnificent noise the whole time; and not a searchlight touched it, as it was the night-out of the Essenden and Luton lights. And not a shot was fired at it. I was amazed at its impunity and audacity. It sailed straight for London and must have got past Hatfield before they woke up and brought it down. The commander was such a splendid personage that the divisional surgeon and an officer who saw him grieved as for an only son. At two o'clock another Zeppelin passed over Ayot; but we have no telephone, and nobody bothered. I went to see the wreck on my motor bicycle. The police were in great feather, as there is a strict cordon, which means that you cant get in without paying. The charges are not excessive, as I guess; for I created a ducal impression by a shilling. Corpses are extra, no doubt; but I did not intrude on the last sleep of the brave. What is hardly cred-ible, but true, is that the sound of the Zepp's engines was so fine, and its voyage through the stars so enchanting, that I positively caught myself hoping next night that there would be another raid. I grieve to add that after seeing the Zepp fall like a burning newspaper, with its human contents roasting for some minutes (it was frightfully slow) I went to bed and was comfortably asleep in ten minutes. One is so pleased at having seen the show that the destruction of a dozen people or so in hideous terror and torment does not count. 'I didnt half cheer, I tell you,' said a damsel at the wreck. Pretty lot of animals we are!

'The Emperor and the Little Girl' (1916)

'Written for the Vestiare Marie-José, a Belgian war charity for children, in 1916' (Shaw's note).

It was one of those nights when you feel nervous and think you see people in the shadows, or even ghosts, because there was a moon, it kept going in and out of the clouds; and a lot of clouds were scurrying across the sky, some so white that you could see the moon through them, others like brown feathers that just dimmed her, and some big dark ones that you knew would blacken out the moon altogether when they caught her. Some people get frightened on such nights and keep indoors in the light and warmth where they are not alone, and the night is shut out by the curtains, but others find themselves very restless, and want to go out and wander about and watch the moon. They like the dark because they can imagine all sorts of things about the places they cant see, and fancy that wonderful kinds of people will come out of the blacknesses and have adventures with them.

On this particular night, it was not half so dangerous to be out in the dark as it had been that afternoon to be out in the light, because it was in one of the places where the English and the French were fighting the Germans. In the day time everyone had to hide in the trenches. If they shewed their heads for a moment: bang! they were shot. There were curtains hung to prevent you from crossing certain fields, only these curtains were not like window curtains: they were really shells, showers of bombshells bursting and digging great holes in the ground, and blowing people and cattle and trees all to bits; so they were called fire curtains. At night there were no fire curtains; and the soldiers who were up all night watching to shoot you could not see you so easily. Still, it was dangerous enough to prevent you imagining ghosts and robbers. Instead, you could not help thinking about the shells and bullets, and about all the dead and wounded men who were still lying where they had been shot. It is not surprising that there was nobody walking about to enjoy the moonlight and to look at the fireworks; for there were fireworks. From time to time the men who were watching to shoot sent up shells that dropped a bright star in the sky, and lit up quite plainly everything and everybody that was in sight on the ground. When this happened, all the men who were stealing about spying on the enemy, or looking for wounded men, or putting up barbed wire fences to protect their trenches, fell flat on their faces and pretended to be dead until the star went out.

Just a little after half-past eleven, in a place where no men were stealing about, and the star shells were all too far off to shew the ground very distinctly, somebody came stalking along in a strange manner; for he was not looking for wounded, nor spying, nor doing any of the things that the soldiers did; he was only wandering about, stopping and then going on again, but never stooping to pick up anything. Sometimes when a star shell came so near that you could see him pretty plainly, he stopped and stood very stiffly upright, and folded his arms. When it was dark again he walked on with a curious striding step, like the step of a very proud man; and yet he had to walk slowly, and watch where he was going, because the ground was all blown into great hollows and pits by bombshells: besides, he might have tripped over a dead soldier. The reason he carried himself so stiffly and haughtily was that he was the German Emperor: if he came at a certain angle between you and the moon or a star shell, you could see the end of his turned up moustache, just as you see it in the pictures. But mostly you could not see him at all; for what with the clouds and most of the star shells being so far off, you very seldom saw anything until you were very close up.

It was so dark that though the Emperor walked very carefully, he stumbled into a great pit, called a crater, made by a mine that had been blown up, and very nearly pitched head foremost to the bottom of it. But he saved himself by clutching at something. He thought it was a tuft of grass; but it was a Frenchman's beard; and the Frenchman was dead. Then the moon came out for a moment; and the Emperor saw that quite a number of soldiers, some French and some German, had been blown up in that mine, and were lying about in the crater. It seemed to him that they were all staring at him.

The Emperor had a dreadful shock. Before he could think of what he was doing he said to the dead men the German words, 'Ich habe es nicht gewollt,' which means, in English, 'It is not my doing,' or 'I never intended to,' or, sometimes, 'It wasnt me': just what you say when you are scolded for doing something wrong. Then he scrambled out of the pit, and walked away from it in another direction. But his inside felt so bad that he had to sit down when he had gone only a little way. At least he could have gone on if he had tried; but an ammunition case which lay in his path was so convenient to sit on, that he thought he would rest until he felt better.

The next thing that happened was very surprising; for a brown thing came out of the darkness; and he would have taken it for a dog if it had not clinked and squeaked as well as made footsteps. When it came nearer he saw that it was a little girl; and she was much too young to be up at a quarter to twelve in the middle of the night. The clinking and squeaking was because she was carrying a tin can. And she was crying, not loudly, but just whimpering. When she saw the Emperor, she was not a bit frightened or surprised: she only stopped crying with a great sniff and sob, and said 'I'm sorry; but all my water is gone.'

'What a pity!' said the Emperor, who was accustomed to children. 'Are you very *very* thirsty? I have a flask, you see; but I'm afraid what is in it would be too strong for you to drink.'

'I dont want to drink,' said the little girl, quite surprised. 'Dont you? Arnt you wounded?'

'No,' said the Emperor. 'What are you crying for?'

The little girl almost began to cry again. 'The soldiers were very unkind to me,' she said, going closer up to the Emperor, and leaning against his knee. 'There are four of them in a mine crater over there. There is a Tommy and a Hairy and two Boches.'

'You must not call a German soldier a Boche,' said the Emperor severely. 'That is very very wrong.'

'No,' said the little girl: 'it is quite right, I assure you. An English soldier is a Tommy; and a French soldier is a Hairy; and a German soldier is a Boche. My mother calls them like that. Everybody does. One of the Boches wears spectacles, and is like a college teacher. The other has been lying out for two nights. None of them can move. They are very bad. I gave them water, and at first they thanked me and prayed that God would bless me, except the college teacher. Then a shell came; and though it was quite far off, they drove me away and said that if I didnt go straight home as fast as I could a bear would come out of the wood and eat me, and my father would beat me with a strap. The college teacher told them out loud that they were softies, and that I didnt matter; but he whispered to me to go home quickly. May I stay with you, please? My father would not beat me, I know: but I am afraid of the bear.'

'You may stay with me,' said the Emperor; 'and I will not let the bear touch you. There really isnt any bear.'

'Are you sure?' said the little girl. 'The Tommy said there was. He said it was a great big bear that boiled little children in his inside after eating them.'

'The English never tell the truth,' said the Emperor.

'He was very kind at first,' said the little girl, beginning to cry again. 'I dont think he would have said it if he didnt believe it, unless the pain of his wound made him fancy things like bears.'

'Dont cry,' said the Emperor. 'He did not mean to be unkind: they were all afraid you would be wounded like themselves, and wanted you to go home so as to be out of danger.'

'Oh, I'm quite used to shells,' said the little girl. 'I go about at night giving water to the wounded, because my father was left lying out for five nights and he suffered dreadfully from thirst.'

'Ich habe es nicht gewollt,' said the Emperor, feeling very sick again.

'Are you a Boche?' said the little girl; for the Emperor had spoken to her before in French. 'You speak French very well; but I thought you were English?'

'I am half English,' said the Emperor.

'Thats funny,' said the little girl. 'You must be very careful; for both sides will try to shoot you.'

The Emperor gave a queer little laugh; and the moon came out and shewed him to the girl more plainly than before. 'You have a very nice cloak, and your uniform is very clean,' she said. 'How can you keep it so clean when you have to lie down in the dirt when a star shell shines?'

'I do not lie down. I stand up. That is how I keep my uniform clean,' said the Emperor.

'But you mustnt stand up,' said the little girl. 'If they see you they will fire at us.'

'Very well, then,' said the Emperor. 'For your sake I will lie down when you are with me; but now you must let me take you home. Where is your house?'

The little girl laughed. 'We havnt a house,' she said. 'First the Germans shelled our village. Then they took it; and the French shelled it. Then the English came and shelled the Germans out of it. Now all three of them shell it. Our house has been struck seven times, and our cowhouse nineteen times. And just fancy: not even the cow was killed. My papa says it has cost 25,000 francs to knock down our cowhouse. He is very proud of it.'

'Ich habe es nicht gewollt,' said the Emperor, coming all over bad again. When he felt better he said, 'Where do you live now?'

'Anywhere we can,' said the girl. 'Oh, it is quite easy: you soon get used to it. What are you? Are you a stretcher bearer?'

'No, my child,' said the Emperor. 'I am what is called a Kaiser.'

'I did not know there was more than one,' said the little girl.

'There are three,' said the Kaiser.

'Do they all have to turn their moustaches up?' said the little girl.

'No,' said the Kaiser. 'They are allowed to wear beards when their moustaches wont turn up.'

'They should put them in curl papers like I do with my hair at Easter,' said the little girl. 'What does a Kaiser do? Does he fight, or does he pick up the wounded?'

'He doesnt exactly *do* anything,' said the Emperor. 'He thinks.'

'What does he think?' said the girl, who like all young things, knew so little about people that when she met them she had to ask them a great many questions, and was sometimes told not to be inquisitive, though her mother usually said, 'Ask no questions, and youll be told no lies.'

'If the Kaiser were to tell, that wouldnt be thinking, would it?' said the Emperor. 'It would be talking.'

'It must be very funny to be a Kaiser,' said the little girl. 'But anyhow, what are you doing here so late when you are not wounded?'

'Will you promise not to tell anybody if I tell you,' said the Emperor. 'It's a secret.'

'I promise faithfully,' said the girl. 'Please do tell me. I love secrets.'

'Then,' said the Emperor, 'I had to tell all my soldiers this morning that I was very sorry I could not go into the trenches and fight under fire as they do, and that the reason was, I had to think hard for them all, that if I were killed they would not know what to do and they would all be beaten and killed.'

'That was very naughty of you,' said the little girl; 'for it wasnt true, you know: was it? When my brother was killed another

38

man just stepped into his place and the battle went on just as if nothing had happened. I think they might have stopped just for a minute; but they didnt. If you were killed, wouldnt somebody step into your place.'

'Yes,' said the Emperor. 'My son would.'

'Then why did you tell them such an awful fib,' said the little girl.

'I was made to,' said the Emperor. 'That is what a Kaiser is for, to be made get up and say things that neither he nor anyone else believes. I saw it in the faces of some of the men today that they didnt believe me, and thought I was a coward making excuses. So when the night came I went to bed and pretended to go asleep; but when they were all gone I got up and stole out here by myself to make sure that I was not afraid. That is why I stand up when the star shells shine.'

'Why not do it in the day time?' said the little girl. 'Thats when the real danger is.'

'They wouldnt let me,' said the Emperor.

'Poor Kaiser!' said the little girl. 'I'm so sorry for you. I hope you wont be wounded. If you are, I'll bring you some water.'

The Emperor felt so fond of her when she said this that he gave her a kiss before he got up and took her by the hand to lead her away to a place of safety. And she felt so fond of him that she never thought of anything else for the moment. This was how it happened that neither of them noticed that a star shell had just lit up right over them, and that the tall figure of the Emperor could be seen by its light from ever so far, though the girl, who was a little thing in a dingy brown dress, and whose face was, to tell the truth, not very clean, looked at a little distance like nothing but an ant heap.

The next moment there was a fearful sound: the sound of a shell rushing through the air so fast that it left the bang of the cannon behind it as it came straight towards them. The Emperor turned round quickly to look; and as he did so two more stars broke out, and another shell began racing towards them from a great distance. And this was a very big one: the Emperor could see it tearing through the air like a great mad elephant, making a noise like a train in a tunnel. The first shell burst not very far away with such a splitting crack that it seemed to be right in the Emperor's ear. And all the time the second shell was coming with a terrible rush.

The Emperor threw himself on his face and clutched the earth with his fists trying to bury himself out of danger. Then he remembered the little girl; and it seemed to him so awful that she should be blown to pieces that he forgot about himself and tried to jump up and throw himself on top of her to shield her.

But you can think of things far quicker than you can do them; and shells are nearly as quick as thinking. Before the Emperor had got his fingers out of the clay, and his knees doubled up to rise there was a most tremendous noise. The Emperor had never heard anything so awful, though he was used to shells at a distance. You couldnt call it a bang, or a roar, or a smash: it was a fearful, tearing, shattering, enormous bang-smash-roar-thunderclap-earthquake sound like the end of the world. The Emperor really believed for a whole minute that he had been blown inside out; for shells do sometimes blow people inside out when they dont actually hit them. When he got up, he did not know whether he was standing on his head or his heels; indeed he was not standing on either; for he fell down again several times. And when at last he managed to keep on his feet by steadying himself against something, he found that the something was a tree that had been quite a long distance away from him when the shell came, so he knew he had been blown all that way by the explosion. And the first thing he said to himself was 'Where is the child?'

'Here,' said a voice in the tree over his head. It was the little girl's voice.

'Gott sei dank!' said the Emperor, greatly relieved, which is the German for 'Thanks be to God!' 'Are you hurt, my child? I thought you were blown to pieces.'

'I *am* blown to pieces,' said the little girl's voice. 'Blown into just two thousand and thirty-seven little tiny weeny pieces. The shell came right into my lap. The biggest bit left is my little toe; its over there nearly half a mile off; one of my thumb nails is over there half a mile the other way; and there are four eyelashes in the crater where the four men have left their bodies; one for each; and one of my front teeth is sticking in the strap of your helmet. But I dont wonder at that, because it was coming loose. All the rest of me is just burnt up and blown into dust.'

'Ich habe es nicht gewollt,' said the Emperor in a voice that would have made anybody pity him. But the little girl didnt pity him at all: she only said:

'Oh, who cares whether you did or not, *now?* I *did* laugh when I saw you flop down on your face in your lovely uniform. I laughed so much that I didnt feel the shell, though it must have given me such a dig. You look funny still, holding on to that tree and swaying about just like Granpapa when he was drunk.'

The Emperor heard her laughing; but what surprised him very much was, he heard other people laughing too, like men with gruff voices.

'Who else is laughing?' he said. 'Is there anyone with you?'

'Oh, lots and lots,' said the voice of the little girl. 'The four men who were in the crater are up here. The first shell set them free.'

'Du hast es nicht gewollt, Willem, was?'[20] said one of the gruff voices; and then all the voices laughed; for it was funny to hear a common soldier call the Emperor Billy.

'You must not deny me the respect you have taught me to consider my due,' said the Emperor. 'I did not make myself Kaiser. You brought me up to it, and denied me the natural equality and innocent play of an ordinary human being. I command you now to treat me as the idol you made me and not as the simple man that God made me.'

'It's no use talking to them,' said the little girl's voice. 'They have all flown away. They didnt care enough about you to

41

listen to you. There is nobody left but me and the Boche in spectacles.'

A man's voice came down from the tree. 'I go not with them because I desire not to associate with soldiers,' it said. 'They know that you made me a professor for telling lies about your grandfather.'

'Fool,' said the Emperor, rudely: 'did you ever tell them the truth about your own grandfather?'

There was no answer; and after a little silence the girl's voice said, 'He has gone away too. I dont believe his grandfather was any better than yours or mine. I think I must go too. I am very sorry; for I used to like you before I was set free by the shell. But now, somehow, you dont seem to matter.'

'My child,' said the Emperor, full of grief at her wanting to leave him. 'I matter as much as I ever did.'

'Yes,' said the little girl's voice: 'but you dont matter to *me*. You never did, you see, except when I was foolish enough to be afraid that you would kill me. I thought it would hurt instead of setting me free. Now that I *am* set free, and it's ever so much nicer than being hungry and cold and frightened, you dont matter a bit. So goodbye.'

'Wait a moment,' said the Emperor in a begging voice. 'There is no hurry; and I'm very lonely.'

'Why dont you make your soldiers fire the big gun at you as they did at me?' said the little girl's voice. 'Then you will be set free, and we can fly about together as you like. Unless you do, I cant stay with you.'

'I may not,' said the Emperor.

'Why not?' said the little girl's voice.

'Because it is not usual,' said the Emperor; 'and the Emperor who does anything unusual is lost, because he is nothing himself but a Usuality.'

'That is a very long word: I never heard it before,' said the little girl's voice. 'Does it mean a clod that cant get away from the earth, no matter how hard it tries?'

'Yes,' said the Emperor. 'Just that.'

'Then we must wait until the Tommies or the Hairies give you a dig with a great shell,' said the little girl's voice. 'Dont be downhearted: I think it very likely they will if you stand up in the light. Now I am going to kiss you goodbye because you kissed me very nicely before I was set free. But I'm afraid you wont be able to feel it.'

And she was quite right; for though the Emperor tried his hardest to feel it he felt nothing. And what made it very tantalizing was that he saw something. For he turned up his face to where the voice came from when she said she would kiss him; and then he saw flying down from the tree the most lovely little rosy body of a tiny girl with wings, perfectly clean and not minding a bit that it had nothing on; and it put its arms round his neck and kissed him before it flew away. He saw it quite distinctly; and this was very curious, because there was no light except dim moonlight in which it should have looked grey or white, like an owl, instead of rosy and pretty. He felt a dreadful pang of grief at parting from her; but it was all spoiled by some real men suddenly speaking to him. He had never noticed them coming. They were two of his officers; and they asked him with great respect whether the shell had hurt him. The little angel disappeared at the first word they spoke. He was so angry at their driving it away that he could not trust himself to speak to them for fully a minute; and then all he said was to ask them rudely the way back to prison. Then, seeing that they did not understand what he meant, and were staring at him as if he were mad, he asked again the way back to his quarters, meaning his tent. They pointed it out: and he strode along in front of them until he reached it, all the sentinels challenging him, and saluting him when the officers answered them. Then he said goodnight, very shortly, and was going in to bed when one of them asked him timidly whether they were to make any report of what had happened. And all the Emperor said was 'You are a couple of — fools,' and the — was a most dreadful swear.

Then they stared at one another, and one of them said, 'The All Highest is as drunk as be —' and that — also was a wicked swear. It was lucky that the Emperor was thinking about the little girl, and did not overhear what the officer said. But it would not really have mattered; for all soldiers use bad words without meaning anything.

'Joy Riding at the Front' (1917)

This extract from What I Really Wrote About the War *(1931) prefaces three articles about visiting the front line that Shaw wrote for* The Daily Chronicle *and published in March 1917.*

Early in 1917 I received an invitation from the British Commander-in-Chief, then Sir Douglas Haig,[21] to visit the front and say my say about it. I felt this as a call, which I was not free to refuse, to such service as I was able to perform in the way of my profession. I equipped myself with a pair of trench boots and a tunic and breeches of khaki, in which I looked neither like a civilian nor a soldier, but in which I was supposed to be invisible to the enemy's marksmen. H.W. Massingham[22] warned me that he had been almost turned back and sent home because the black of his civilian clothes shewed for an inch beneath his khaki trench overcoat. H.G. Wells told me to take waders, as I should have to walk kneedeep through the Flanders mud.

When I arrived on the field of battle I found that these precautions were entirely wasted. Flanders was virgin white in its mantle of snow. The temperature averaged about 17°F.; and I came home without a speck of mud on the trench boots. At the Pozières windmill I was in the company of a Roumanian General in very smart dove color, with a cap beside which the most gorgeous macaw would have looked like a London sparrow. His son was of the party and looked almost as conspicuous. C.E. Montague,[23] who was in responsible charge of us, stopped when a shell burst half a mile away, and remonstrated. 'But,' said the General, 'on the snow it is I who am invisible, whilst you two gentlemen [Montague and Shaw] are conspicuous in your khaki.' This was so obviously true that Montague had to shrug his shoulders and lead on.

The German artillerists took no advantage of the situation as far as I was concerned. The battle seemed to me unaccountably onesided. Our guns worked away industriously, the heaven-rending energy of the guns and the whizzing rush of the shells contrasting quaintly with the languid boredom of the gunners as they screwed in the fuses, hoisted the shells into the guns, and pulled the string, letting another steel comet loose in space without a pretence of conviction that it would arrive anywhere in particular or of concern as to whether it did or not. At first I expected their efforts to provoke a thundering retaliative cannonade from the embattled central empires, an expectation which gained a mild thrill from the possibility that their first efforts to find the range might land on my epigastrium; but no: our bombardment did not elicit a single remonstrance: it was like the imaginary battles of my childhood, in which I was always victorious and the enemy fell before my avenging sword without getting in a single blow. I demanded explanations. The first reply was, 'Oh, they have not been doing much counter battery work lately.' Another was, 'They will start firing on Albert at three o'clock.' Nobody knew the truth, which was that the Germans had retreated quietly to the Hindenburg line[24] and left us to waste our ammunition on their empty trenches. In short, the Somme battle field was very much safer than the Thames Embankment with its race of motors and trams. Only in Ypres and perhaps in Arras could I flatter myself that I was to any perceptible extent under fire. I did not see yellow as Goethe did on the field of Valmy and Wagner in the Dresden insurrection.[25] I suffered much more from funk during the air raids in London, where I was too lazy to leave my bed and take refuge in the cellars or the nearest underground railway station, as the more energetic citizens did.

I recall one moment of apparent peril as shewing how unconscious men may be of their instinctive actions. The Commander-in-Chief had taken me with him to see a great display of the latest contrivances in flame projection, incendiary showers of thermit, and poison gas discharge. The thermit shower was produced by firing from Stokes guns[26] a cloud of shells packed with it. I was standing with Haig amid an imposing group of officers on a highway, beside which the ground dropped straight down to an emplacement seven or eight feet below, on which were ranged the Stokes guns; so that they were right under our noses. Their first volley was a wonder of pyrotechny: it produced a vast curtain of white incandescence of dazzling brilliancy, and – at least so we were assured – of such incredibly high temperature that hell itself would have shrivelled up in it. This sounded impressive; but the older officers were contemptuous, declaring that the stuff cooled so suddenly that you could pick it up when it touched ground and put it in your pocket 'like a fourpenny bit' (a coin I had not seen since early childhood) with perfect impunity. Nevertheless the military love of display insisted on a second volley; and this time one of the guns immediately beneath us, instead of hurling its fiery shell joyously into the skies, gave a sickly cough and tossed it about twenty feet up, from which eminence it began returning to the toes of the gunner, where it seemed inevitable that it must explode and consume us all like stubble.

Now on the evidence of my own senses I am prepared to swear that neither I nor any of that dignified group of commanding officers budged an inch. Our *tenue* was splendidly undisturbed: the example we set of heroic imperturbability in danger was perfect. Only, I noticed that we were now all at the other side of the road. On the evidence of that fact we must have scuttled like rabbits. On the evidence of my own consciousness I had not flinched; and the others certainly looked as if they had stood like statues. Fortunately the shell had not exploded: it was a dud. I can only hope that I did not head the retreat.

The flame projection was very horrible: the contents of a huge array of barrels of kerosene swept through a half circle of about 80 feet radius, devouring everything there in an ugly stinking rush of smoke and murky fire. But as it must have taken at least twenty-four hours to build up the contrivance, which was a clumsy affair after all, I privately concluded that it was neither practical in the face of an active enemy nor worth while. The portable flame throwers, about which recent German experiments had made Haig anxious, were obviously first attempts, hopeless except as instruments for self-cremation. Even the poison gas shewed its most obvious limitation when an officer came up to Haig and apologized for having exhibited only two clouds of it (they were white and visible) his excuse being that any more would be a little hard on the two friendly villages towards which they were drifting.

On the Death of Mrs Patrick Campbell's Son (1918)

Shaw wrote his letter to the famous actress on 7th January 1918. Mrs Campbell (1865–1940) had starred as Eliza Doolittle in Pygmalion *just before the war. Her son, Alan Hugh Campbell, was killed at the end of December 1917.*

Never saw it or heard about it [the death of her son] until your letter came. It is no use: I cant be sympathetic: these things simply make me furious. I want to swear. I *do* swear. Killed just because people are blasted fools. A chaplain, too, to say nice things about it. It is not his business to say nice things about it, but to shout that 'the voice of thy son's blood crieth unto God from the ground.'[27]

To hell with your chaplain and his tragic gentleness! The next shell will perhaps blow *him* to bits; and some other chaplain will write such a nice letter to *his* mother. Such nice letters! Such nice little notices in papers!

Gratifying, isnt it. Consoling. It only needs a letter from the king to make me feel that the shell was a blessing in disguise.

No: dont show me the letter. But I should very much like to have a nice talk with that dear chaplain, that sweet sky pilot, that –

No use going on like this, Stella. Wait for a week; and then I shall be very clever and broadminded again, and have forgotten all about him. I shall be quite as nice as the chaplain.

Oh damn, damn, damn, damn, damn, damn, damn, damn, DAMN

DAMN!

And oh, dear, dear, dear, dear, dear, dearest!

War Issues for Irishmen: An Open Letter to Col. Arthur Lynch from Bernard Shaw (1918)

Shaw wrote this pamphlet at the request of the Irish recruiting authorities, and addressed it to Col. Arthur Lynch (1861–1934), who was once convicted of treason for his pro-Boer activities, and who later became Nationalist MP for West Clare, Ireland. The armistice was declared just as the pamphlet was to be published.

To ask Irishmen to die for freedom is one thing: to ask them to die in order that Lords Curzon[28] and Milner may get the upper hand of the Hohenzollern dynasty is another. It is silly to pretend that the governing classes of Europe can be unanimous in desiring to make the world safe for Democracy. There is something revolting in the democratic professions of politicians whose whole career flatly contradicts the notion that they are fighting to overthrow the social order which they have always defended, and which is in all essentials the same in the Central Empires as in their present enemies. It was evident in 1914 that on most questions which divide the interests of the man of the people, Irish or English, from those of the governing classes, the figureheads of the Allies sympathized with the Kaiser and not with the figureheads of proletarian democracy. It is still evident that their opinions and interests have not changed. They govern in the interests of the country house and the counting house, regarding labor as a source of rent for the one and profit for the other. As between King William Hohenzollern and Mr Arthur James Balfour,[29] dominated as they both are by the economic interests and social ideas and traditions of their class, there is, from the point of view of the man who lives by labor, nothing to choose. It is not possible to believe that Mr Balfour feels otherwise on the Irish question than the Kaiser on the Polish question.

I do not see how recruits can be gained in Ireland by shirking these considerations. They are obvious to all neutral and detached nations; and Ireland is not only neutral and detached, but hostile and critical where England is concerned. Whoever is to recruit effectively in Ireland must put all these cards frankly on the table. The Irish may be persuaded to enlist, or forced into the army as slave soldiers; but they will not be humbugged into enlisting by the rhetoric of British patriotism...

What we Irish have to consider, then, is not what the kings and their councillors and their warriors intended this war to be, but what, in the hands of that inexorable Power of whom it used to be said that 'Man proposes: God disposes,' it has now actually become over and above its merely horrible aspect as an insane killing match. If there is anything at stake except military prestige, and the resulting Overbalance of Power, what is it? I think we must reply that the war has become a phase of that great struggle towards equality as the sole effective guarantee of democracy and liberty which is being constantly waged against the delivery of human welfare into the custody and control of privileged persons and classes: in short, against robbery of the poor and idolatry of the rich...

So far it is plain that the Irish side is for once the side on which the English find themselves; and the English generals naturally want Irish soldiers because, though they do not like them, and resent the detachment and frank derision with which they regard British moral pretensions in respect of nationalities struggling to be free and so forth, they know their value as soldiers and are anxious to have an Irish element in every battalion. Why does the Irishman hold back?

Not, clearly, that he is more afraid of being killed than other people: he is actually sought for because he raises the standard of military courage in the field under the spur of his insurgent national pride, as the Irish casualties shew. Not, either, in any number of cases worth reckoning because he wants Germany to win with a view to the German terms of peace including the establishment of Ireland as an independent nation, like Belgium or Greece, under the guarantee of the victorious Central Empires. This was Roger Casement's plan;[30] but it is too technical politically for anyone but a professional diplomatist like Casement to understand; and the ruthless exposure by the war of the utter dependence of Belgium and Greece on their ruthless guarantors, and the uselessness of the 'scraps of paper' which guaranteed them, ought by this time to have set every intelligent Irishman implacably against such skull-grinning Independence as that.

The common Irishman takes a simpler view. He regards England as Ireland's enemy; and his conclusion is that England's enemies are his friends. This is natural logic; but it is bad logic. The Chinese pirate is the Englishman's enemy; but if the Irishman were on that account to depend on the friendship of the Chinese pirate, or even to refrain from very strenuously helping the Englishman to hang him, he would probably have his throat cut for his sulkiness. The Englishman and the Frenchman fight with what help they can get: Japanese, Negro, Red Indian, Pathan, Senegalese (none of them bosom friends of white men, to say the least) are good enough for them when they have a common foe to overcome. An Irishman who will not fight for his side in the world conflict because the English are fighting on that side too has no political sense; and an Ireland composed of such men could never be free, even if the gates of freedom were open wide before her. It is a case not of refusing to help the English in a bad cause, but of refusing to take advantage of the help of the English in a good one.

Then there is the more intelligent Irishman who hopes that the war may end in the establishment of a League of Nations, and that this League may take up the Irish question and insist on Ireland having its place as a nation, and not remaining a conquered territory governed by her conqueror. America, he thinks, may have a good deal to say in the matter on behalf of Ireland. She may have more if Ireland takes a generous share in the war. But we must not deceive ourselves as to the interest the rest of the world takes in our little island and our little people. Those of us who talk and think as if, outside England, all the great federations, empires, and nations of the world were enthusiastic branches of the Gaelic League, or that they will put Irish interests before their own lightest advantage in the settlement after the war, or that they care twopence more for Ireland than they do for Poland, Finland, Bohemia, Armenia, or any of the Jugo-Slav conquests of Austria, are deceiving themselves very ridiculously. The truth is that these great European and Asiatic Powers will be hardly conscious of Ireland when the settlement comes. We are too far out of their way. We shall count for less with them in the treaty than Cyprus did in the Treaty of Berlin.[31] We can make England feel us; and America is well aware of us; but we cannot make Europe feel us. The beginning of diplomatic wisdom with us is to realize our own insignificance outside the group of islands to which we belong. But if we have no diplomatic importance, our sentimental importance in America and the Overseas Dominions, and our political importance within the British Islands, is considerable: it is, in fact, out of all proportion to our merits. And if Sinn Fein is to mean anything but organized national selfishness and insularity, it must take serious count of English and American sympathy. If I say that the Irish people are under very strong obligations to the English people, obligations which it would be the grossest ingratitude to deny or forget, I shall no doubt astonish those bookmade Irish patriots who are too busy reading about the Treaty of Limerick and the feats of Brian Boru[32] to see anything that happens under their noses. But at least they must be dimly conscious that there was an attempt made in Dublin in the Easter of 1916 to establish an independent Irish Republic, and that one of its leaders was a noted Socialist Trade Unionist named James Connolly who, being captured by the British troops, was denied the right of a prisoner of war, and shot.[33] Now Connolly owed his position and influence as an Irish National leader to the part he had taken in organizing the great strike of the transport workers in Dublin in 1913; and the remains of his organization was the nucleus of the little army of the Irish Republican Brotherhood. That strike was sustained for many months after it would have exhausted the resources of the Irish workers had they not been aided from abroad. Where did the aid come from? From the reckless generosity of the English unions. The English workers fed, out of their own scanty wages, the Irish strikers and their families for months. I myself, with Connolly and Mr George Russell, was among the speakers at a huge meeting got up in aid of the strike by Mr James Larkin in London.[34] It was a genuine non-party meeting called by English workers and crowded by thousands of English people, who rallied to the Irish strike with unbounded enthusiasm and with as much money as they could afford, and indeed more than they would have thrown away on that doomed struggle if their heads had been as clear as their sympathies were warm. Connolly got the money by the plea that the cause of Labor was the same cause all the world over, and that as against the idler and the profiteer England and Ireland were 'members one of another'. We did not set up the cry of Sinn Fein then. We did not say 'WE OURSELVES are sufficient to ourselves: you can keep your English money and leave us to take care of ourselves.' We took the money and were glad to get it and spend it. We cannot now with any decency forget Connolly and change the subject to Cromwell and General Maxwell.[35] I have the right to remind the Irish people of this, because I was one of those who asked for the money; and I was cheered to the echo by Englishmen and Englishwomen for doing so. I am an Irishman; and I have not forgotten English working-class mothers have the right to say to me: 'Our sons are in the trenches, fighting for their lives and liberties and for yours; and some of your sons who took our money when they were starving are leaving them to fight alone.' Not a very heroic position, that, for an Irish movement which is always talking heroics...

Let me turn now from the broad unselfish view to the narrow and interested one; for it is useless to pretend that lads brought up as so many of ours have been, drudging for mean wages on small farms in petty parishes, can be expected to reason like statesmen or to feel obliged to repay benefits that came directly only to workers in cities they never set foot in. To them you must say that horrible as this war is, it has raised millions of men and their families from a condition not far above savagery to comparative civilization. A trench is a safer place than a Dublin slum; and the men in it are well fed, well clothed, and certain that, whatever the Germans may do to them, at least their own commanders are keenly interested in the preservation of their lives and the maintenance of their health and strength, which is more than can be said of their employers at home. Their wives get a separation allowance; and the children are considered and allowed for too. The huge sums of money that this costs are taken largely from the incomes of rich landlords and capitalists who have to give up one pound out of every three they possess to feed, clothe, and equip the soldier, and keep his wife at home. The wonder is that any man chooses to live in a slum or drudge as a laborer on a farm when he can get into the army. But at least, some of them will say, you do not get blown to bits by high-explosive shells in a slum. Unfortunately, you do. Bombs are raining on civilian slums, farmhouses, and cottages every day in this war; and the rain gets heavier from week to week. If the slums of Ireland have escaped so far, it is only because the slums of England are nearer to the German lines; and the day is not far distant when, if the war goes on, the soldier in his bomb-proof dug-out will be safer from shells than the slum dweller in his wretched room. The aeroplane and the torpedo are making short work of the safety of the civilian in war.

Then take the case of the lad on the farm. He knows nothing of the world: his only taste of adventure is pretending to be a soldier by doing a little precarious illegal drilling which teaches him nothing of real modern warfare, though it may easily tempt him to throw away his life in a hopeless rising of men fed on dreams against men armed with tanks and aeroplanes. His wages would be spat at by a dock laborer in a British port; and the farmer keeps them down by employing his own sons as laborers for a few shillings pocket money. He is under everyone's thumb; yet he is afraid of military discipline, which, severe as it is, yet has limits beyond which the soldier is reasonably free, and even unreasonably free, whereas a laborer is never free at all. The laborer is never sure of his food from week to week; but in military service he never has to think about this: food, lodging, and clothing are provided for him as certainly as they are for a general, in return for a round of duties which, though the slightest neglect or slackness in performing them is fiercely punished, are, taking one year with another, neither as heavy nor as wearing as the never ending jobs of an agricultural laborer. In many branches of the service, such as the air force and artillery, there is valuable mechanical training to be had; and even the physical training of the ordinary infantry soldier pulls the country lad together and smartens him up, besides forcing him to do things that must be done promptly and to make up his mind instead of mooning. Travelling and the sight of foreign countries and contact with foreign peoples, which form an essential and expensive part of the education of a gentleman, can be obtained by an Irish country lad in no other way than through military service. Now that the service is compulsory in England the soldier finds himself in ordinary respectable company, often better than he has ever been in before. I am not playing the tricks of the recruiting sergeant and trying to persuade Irish lads that a soldier's life is all beer and skittles. If it has opportunities and advantages, it has also dangers and hardships which are inevitable; and it has injustices and cruelties which are all the harder to bear as they are mostly stupid and mischievous relics of the days when soldiers were the dregs of the population. But if an Irish agricultural laborer compares the soldier's condition, not with a condition of ideal happiness and freedom, but with his own, he will think twice before missing such a chance as the war offers him of seeing a little more of the world than the half dozen fields and the village public house which now imprison him. When one considers what the daily life of four out of every five young Irishmen is, one wonders that more laborers do not jump at the chance the new army offers them.

Heartbreak House, Preface (1919)

The play itself was not produced until 1920 in New York and 1921 in London.

'Straining at the gnat and swallowing the camel'
There was a frivolous exultation in death for its own sake, which was at bottom an inability to realize that the deaths were real deaths and not stage ones. Again and again, when an air raider dropped a bomb which tore a child and its mother limb from limb, the people who saw it, though they had been reading with great cheerfulness of thousands of such happenings day after day in their newspapers, suddenly burst into furious imprecations on 'the Huns' as murderers, and shrieked for

savage and satisfying vengeance. At such moments it became clear that the deaths they had not seen meant no more to them than the mimic deaths of the cinema screen. Sometimes it was not necessary that death should be actually witnessed: it had only to take place under circumstances of sufficient novelty and proximity to bring it home almost as sensationally and effectively as if it had been actually visible.

For example, in the spring of 1915 there was an appalling slaughter of our young soldiers at Neuve Chapelle and at the Gallipoli landing.[36] I will not go so far as to say that our civilians were delighted to have such exciting news to read at breakfast. But I cannot pretend that I noticed either in the papers, or in general intercourse, any feeling beyond the usual one that the cinema show at the front was going splendidly, and that our boys were the bravest of the brave. Suddenly there came the news that an Atlantic liner, the Lusitania, had been torpedoed, and that several well-known first class passengers, including a famous theatrical manager and the author of a popular farce, had been drowned, among others. The others included Sir Hugh Lane; but as he had only laid the country under great obligations in the sphere of the fine arts, no great stress was laid on that loss.[37]

Immediately an amazing frenzy swept through the country. Men who up to that time had kept their heads now lost them utterly. 'Killing saloon passengers! What next?' was the essence of the whole agitation; but it is far too trivial a phrase to convey the faintest notion of the rage which possessed us. To me, with my mind full of the hideous cost of Neuve Chapelle, Ypres, and the Gallipoli landing, the fuss about the Lusitania seemed almost a heartless impertinence, though I was well acquainted personally with the three best-known victims, and understood, better perhaps than most people, the misfortune of the death of Lane. I even found a grim satisfaction, very intelligible to all soldiers, in the fact that the civilians who found the war such splendid British sport should get a sharp taste of what it was to the actual combatants. I expressed my impatience very freely, and found that my very straightforward and natural feeling in the matter was received as a monstrous and heartless paradox. When I asked those who gaped at me whether they had anything to say about the holocaust of Festubert,[38] they gaped wider than before, having totally forgotten it, or rather, having never realized it. They were not heartless any more than I was; but the big catastrophe was too big for them to grasp, and the little one had been just the right size for them. I was not surprised. Have I not seen a public body for just the same reason pass a vote for £30,000 without a word, and then spend three special meetings, prolonged into the night, over an item of seven shillings for refreshments?

'Little minds and big battles'
Nobody will be able to understand the vagaries of public feeling during the war unless they bear constantly in mind that the war in its entire magnitude did not exist for the average civilian. He could not conceive even a battle, much less a campaign. To the suburbs the war was nothing but a suburban squabble. To the miner and navvy it was only a series of bayonet fights between German champions and English ones. The enormity of it was quite beyond most of us. Its episodes had to be reduced to the dimensions of a railway accident or a shipwreck before it could produce any effect on our minds at all. To us the ridiculous bombardments of Scarborough and Ramsgate were colossal tragedies, and the battle of Jutland a mere ballad.[39] The words 'after thorough artillery preparation' in the news from the front meant nothing to us; but when our seaside trippers learned that an elderly gentleman at breakfast in a week-end marine hotel had been interrupted by a bomb dropping into his egg-cup, their wrath and horror knew no bounds. They declared that this would put a new spirit into the army, and had no suspicion that the soldiers in the trenches roared with laughter over it for days, and told each other that it would do the blighters at home good

to have a taste of what the army was up against. Sometimes the smallness of view was pathetic. A man would work at home regardless of the call 'to make the world safe for democracy'. His brother would be killed at the front. Immediately he would throw up his work and take up the war as a family blood feud against the Germans. Sometimes it was comic. A wounded man, entitled to his discharge, would return to the trenches with a grim determination to find the Hun who had wounded him and pay him out for it.

It is impossible to estimate what proportion of us, in khaki or out of it, grasped the war and its political antecedents as a whole in the light of any philosophy of history or knowledge of what war is. I doubt whether it was as high as our proportion of higher mathematicians. But there can be no doubt that it was prodigiously outnumbered by the comparatively ignorant and childish. Remember that these people had to be stimulated to make the sacrifices demanded by the war, and that this could not be done by appeals to a knowledge which they did not possess, and a comprehension of which they were incapable. When the armistice at last set me free to tell the truth about the war at the following general election, a soldier said to a candidate whom I was supporting 'If I had known all that in 1914, they would never have got me into khaki.' And that, of course, was precisely why it had been necessary to stuff him with a romance that any diplomatist would have laughed at. Thus the natural confusion of ignorance was increased by a deliberately propagated confusion of nursery bogey stories and melodramatic nonsense, which at last overreached itself and made it impossible to stop the war before we had not only achieved the triumph of vanquishing the German army and thereby overthrowing its militarist monarchy, but made the very serious mistake of ruining the centre of Europe, a thing that no sane European State could afford to do.

Saint Joan, Preface (1924)

Joan's trial in scene six provides the climax to the play (produced in New York in 1923 and in 1924 in London). Shaw's Preface raises issues surrounding Joan's trial as well as providing contemporary parallels.

A trial by Joan's French partisans would have been as unfair as the trial by her French opponents; and an equally mixed tribunal would have produced a deadlock. Such recent trials as those of Edith Cavell[40] by a German tribunal and Roger Casement by an English one were open to the same objection; but they went forward to the death nevertheless, because neutral tribunals were not available. Edith, like Joan, was an arch heretic: in the middle of the war she declared before the world that 'Patriotism is not enough.' She nursed enemies back to health, and assisted their prisoners to escape, making it abundantly clear that she would help any fugitive or distressed person without asking whose side he was on, and acknowledging no distinction before Christ between Tommy and Jerry and Pitou the *poilu*.[41] Well might Edith have wished that she could bring the Middle Ages back, and have fifty civilians, learned in the law or vowed to the service of God, to support two skilled judges in trying her case according to the Catholic law of Christendom, and to argue it out with her at sitting after sitting for many weeks. The modern military Inquisition was not so squeamish. It shot her out of hand; and her countrymen, seeing in this a good opportunity for lecturing the enemy on his intolerance, put up a statue to her, but took particular care not to inscribe on the pedestal 'Patriotism is not enough,' for which omission, and the lie it implies, they will need Edith's intercession when they are themselves brought to judgment, if any heavenly power thinks such moral cowards capable of pleading to an intelligible indictment...

The degree of tolerance attainable at any moment depends on the strain under which society is maintaining its cohesion. In war, for instance, we suppress the gospels and put Quakers in prison, muzzle the newspapers, and make it a serious offence to shew a light at night. Under the strain of invasion the French Government in 1792 struck off 4,000 heads, mostly on grounds that would not in time of settled peace have provoked any Government to chloroform a dog; and in 1920 the British Government slaughtered and burnt in Ireland to persecute the advocates of a constitutional change which it had presently to effect itself. Later on the Fascisti in Italy did everything that the Black and Tans did in Ireland,[42] with some grotesquely ferocious variations, under the strain of an unskilled attempt at industrial revolution by Socialists who understood Socialism even less than Capitalists understand Capitalism. In the United States an incredibly savage persecution of Russians took place during the scare spread by the Russian Bolshevik revolution after 1917. These instances could easily be multiplied; but they are enough to shew that between a maximum of indulgent toleration and a ruthlessly intolerant Terrorism there is a scale through which toleration is continually rising or falling... The Inquisition, with its English equivalent the Star Chamber, are gone in the sense that their names are now disused; but can any of the modern substitutes for the Inquisition, the Special Tribunals and Commissions, the punitive expeditions, the suspensions of the Habeas Corpus Act, the proclamations of martial law and of minor states of siege, and the rest of them, claim that their victims have as fair a trial, as well considered a body of law to govern their cases, or as conscientious a judge to insist on strict legality of procedure as Joan had from the Inquisition and from the spirit of the Middle Ages even when her country was under the heaviest strain of civil and foreign war? From us she would have had no trial and no law except a Defence of The Realm Act suspending all law; and for judge she would have had, at best, a bothered major, and at worst a promoted advocate in ermine and scarlet to whom the scruples of a trained ecclesiastic like Cauchon would seem ridiculous and ungentlemanly.[43]

If the British Empire were the only State on earth, the process [of empire building] might go on peacefully (except for ordinary police coercion) until the whole earth was civilized under the British flag. This is the dream of British Imperialism. But it is not what the world is like. There are all the other States, large and small, with their Imperialist dreamers and their very practical traders pushing for foreign markets, and their navies and armies to back the traders and annex these markets. Sooner or later, as they push their boundaries into Africa and Asia, they come up against one another. A collision of that kind (called the Fashoda incident)[44] very nearly involved us in a war with France. Fortunately France gave way, not being prepared to fight us just then; but France and Britain were left with the whole Sudan divided between them. France had before this pushed into and annexed Algeria and (virtually) Tunisia; and Spain was pushing into Morocco. Italy, alarmed lest there should be nothing left for her, made a dash at Tripoli and annexed it. England was in Egypt as well as in India. Now imagine yourself for a moment a German trader, with more goods than you can sell in Germany, having either to shut up your factory and be ruined, or find a foreign market in Africa. Imagine yourself looking at the map of Africa. The entire Mediterranean coast, the pick of the basket, is English, Italian, French, and Spanish. The Hinterland, as you call it, is English and French. You cannot get in anywhere without going through the English Suez Canal or round the Cape to some remote place down south. Do you now understand what the German Kaiser meant when he complained that Germany had not been left 'a place in the sun'? That hideous war of 1914–18 was at bottom a fight between the capitalists of England, France, and Italy on the one side, and those of Germany on the other, for command of the African markets. On top, of course, it was about other things: about Austria making the murder of the Archduke[45] a pretext for subjugating Serbia; about Russia mobilizing against Austria to prevent this; about Germany being dragged into the Austro-Russian quarrel by her alliance with Austria; about France being dragged in on the other side by her alliance with Russia; about the German army having to make a desperate attempt to conquer the French army before the Russian troops could reach her; about England having to attack Germany because she was allied to France and Russia; and about the German army having taken the shortest cut through Belgium, not knowing that Belgium had a secret arrangement with England to have a British expedition sent to defend her if Germany invaded her. Of course the moment the first shot was fired all the Britons and Belgians and Germans and French and Austrians and Russians became enraged sheep, and imagined all sorts of romantic reasons for fighting, in addition to the solid reason that if Tommy and the Poilu and Ivan did not kill Hans and Fritz, Hans and Fritz would kill Tommy and the Poilu and Ivan. Before the killing had gone on very long, the Turks, the Bulgarians, the Japanese, the Americans, and other States that had no more to do with the first quarrel than you had, were in it and at it hammer and tongs. The whole world went mad, and never alluded to markets except when they ridiculed the Kaiser for his demand for a place in the sun.

Yet there would have been no war without the alliances; and the alliances could not have fought if they had not set up great armaments, especially the new German navy, to protect their foreign markets and frontiers. These armaments, created to produce a sense of security, had produced a sense of terror in which no nation dared go unarmed unless it was too small to have any chance against the great Powers, and could depend on their jealousy of oneanother to stave off a conquest by any one of them. Soon the nations that dared not go unarmed became more terrified still, and dared not go alone: they had to form alliances and go in twos and threes, like policemen in thieves' quarters, Germany and Austria in one group and England, France, and Russia in another, both trying to induce Italy and Turkey and America to join them. Their differences were not about their own countries: the German navy was not built to bombard Portsmouth nor the British navy to bombard Bremerhaven. But when the German navy interfered in the north of Africa, which was just what it was built for, and the French and British navies frightened it off from that market in the sun, the capitalist diplomatists of these nations saw that the first thing to concentrate on was not the markets but the sinking of the German navy by the combined French and British navies (or vice versa) on any available pretext. And as you cannot have fleets fighting on the sea without armies fighting on the land to help them, the armies grew like the fleets; the Race of Armaments became as familiar as the Derby; all the natural and kindly sentiments of white civilized nations towards oneanother were changed into blustering terror, the parent of hatred, malice, and all uncharitableness; and after all, when the explosive mixture blew up at last, and blew millions of us with it, it was not about the African markets, but about a comparatively trumpery quarrel between Austria and Serbia which the other Powers could have settled with the greatest ease, without the shedding of one drop of blood, if they had been on decent human terms with oneanother instead of on competitive capitalistic terms.

And please do not fail to note that whereas in the early days of Capitalism our capitalists did not compel us to fight for their markets with our own hands, but hired German serfs and British voluntary professional soldiers for the job, their wars have now become so colossal that every woman's husband, father, son, brother, or sweetheart, if young and strong enough to carry a rifle, must go to the trenches as helplessly as cattle go to the slaughterhouse, abandoning wife and children, home and business, and renouncing normal morality and humanity, pretending all the time that such conduct is splendid and heroic and that his name will live for ever, though he may have the greatest horror of war, and be perfectly aware that the enemy's soldiers, against whom he is defending his hearth, are in exactly the same predicament as himself, and would never dream of injuring him or his if the pressure of the drive for markets were removed from both.

I have purposely brought you to the question of war because your conscience must be sorely troubled about it. You have seen the men of Europe rise up and slaughter oneanother in the most horrible manner in millions. Your son, perhaps, has received a military cross for venturing into the air in a flying machine and dropping a bomb on a sleeping village, blowing several children into fragments, and mutilating or killing their parents. From a militarist, nationalist, or selfishly patriotic point of view such deeds may appear glorious exploits; but from the point of view of any universally valid morality: say from the point of view of a God who is the father of Englishmen and Germans, Frenchmen and Turks alike, they must seem outbursts of the most infernal wickedness. As such they have caused many of us to despair of human nature. A bitter cynicism has succeeded to transports of pugnacious hatred of which all but the incorrigibly thoughtless, and a few incurables who have been mentally disabled for life by the war fever, are now heartily ashamed. I can hardly believe that you have escaped your share of this crushing disillusion. If you are human as well as intelligent you must feel about your species very much as the King of Brobdingnag did when he took Gulliver in his hand as a child takes a tin soldier, and heard his boastful patriotic discourse about the glories of military history.[46]

Perhaps I can console you a little. If you will look at the business in the light of what we have just been studying I think you will see that the fault lay not so much in our characters as in the capitalist system which we had allowed to dominate our lives until it became a sort of blind monster which neither we nor the capitalists could control. It is absurd to pretend that the young men of Europe ever wanted to hunt each other into holes in the ground and throw bombs into the holes to disembowel one-another, or to have to hide in those holes themselves, eaten with lice and sickened by the decay of the unburied, in unutterable discomfort, boredom, and occasionally acute terror, or that any woman ever wanted to put on her best Sunday clothes and be gratified at the honor done to her son for killing some other woman's babies. The capitalists and their papers try to persuade themselves and us that we are like that and always will be, in spite of all the Christmas cards and Leagues of Nations. It is not a bit true. The staggering fact about all these horrors was that we found ourselves compelled to do them in spite of the fact that they were so unintended by us, and so repugnant and dreadful to us that, when at last the war suddenly stopped, our heroic pretences dropped from us like blown-off hats, and we danced in the streets for weeks, mad with joy, until the police had to stop us to restore the necessary traffic. We still celebrate, by two minutes' national silence, not the day on which the glorious war broke out, but the day on which the horrible thing came to an end. Not the victory, which we have thrown away by abusing it as helplessly as we fought for it, but the Armistice, the Cessation, the stoppage of the Red Cross vans from the terminuses of the Channel railways with their heartbreaking loads of mutilated men, was what we danced for so wildly and pitifully. If ever there was anything made clear in the world it was that we were no more directly guilty of the war than we were guilty of the earthquake of Tokio. We and the French and the Germans and the Turks and the rest found ourselves conscripted for an appalling slaughtering match, ruinous to ourselves, ruinous to civilization, and so dreaded by the capitalists themselves that it was only by an extraordinary legal suspension of all financial obligations (called the Moratorium) that the City was induced to face it. The attempt to fight out the war with volunteers failed: there were not enough. The rest went because they were forced to go, and fought because they were forced to fight. The women let them go partly because they could not help themselves, partly because they were just as pugnacious as the men, partly because they read the papers (which were not allowed to tell them the truth), and partly because most of them were so poor that they grasped at the allowances which left most of them better off with their husbands in the trenches than they had ever been with their husbands at home.

How had they got into this position? Simply by the original sin of allowing their countries to be moved and governed and fed and clothed by the pursuit of profit for capitalists instead of by the pursuit of righteous prosperity for 'all people that on earth do dwell'. The first ship that went to Africa to sell things to the natives at more than cost price because there was no sale for them at home began not only this war, but the other and worse wars that will follow it if we persist in depending on Capitalism for our livelihood and our morals. All these monstrous evils begin in a small and apparently harmless way. It is not too much to say that when a nation, having five shillings to divide-up, gives four to Fanny and one to Sarah instead of giving half a crown to each and seeing that she earns it, it sows the seed of all the evils that now make thoughtful and farseeing men speak of our capitalistic civilization as a disease instead of a blessing.

'This Danger of War' (1937)

Shaw broadcast this address on the BBC on 2nd November 1937.

What about this danger of war which is making us all shake in our shoes at present? I am like yourself; I have an intense objection to having my house demolished by a bomb from an aeroplane and myself killed in a horribly painful way by mustard gas. I have visions of streets heaped with mangled corpses, in which children wander crying for their parents, and babies gasp and strangle in the clutches of dead mothers. That is what war means nowadays. It is what is happening in Spain and in China whilst I speak to you,[47] and it may happen to us tomorrow. And the worst of it is that it does not matter two straws to Nature, the mother of us all, how dreadfully we misbehave ourselves in this way or in what hideous agonies we die. Nature can produce children enough to make good any extremity of slaughter of which we are capable. London may be destroyed, Paris, Rome, Berlin, Vienna, Constantinople may be laid in smoking ruins, and the last shrieks of their women and children may give way to the silence of death. No matter. Nature will replace the dead. She is doing so every day. The new men will replace the old cities, and perhaps come to the same miserable end. To Nature the life of an empire is no more than the life of a swarm of bees, and a thousand years are of less account than half an hour to you and me. Now, the moral of that is that we must not depend on any sort of Divine Providence to put a stop to war. Providence says: 'Kill oneanother, my children. Kill oneanother to your hearts' content. There are plenty more where you came from.' Consequently, if we want the war to stop we must all become conscientious objectors.

I dislike war not only for its dangers and inconveniences, but because of the loss of so many young men, any of whom may be a Newton or an Einstein, a Beethoven, a Michael Angelo, a Shakespear, or even a Shaw. Or he may be what is of much more immediate importance, a good baker or a good weaver or builder. If you think of a pair of combatants as a heroic British Saint Michael bringing the wrath of God upon a German Lucifer, then you may exult in the victory of Saint Michael if he kills Lucifer or burn to avenge him if his dastardly adversary mows him down with a machine gun before he can get to grips with him. In that way you can get intense emotional experience from war. But suppose you think of the two as they probably are, say two good carpenters, taken away from their proper work to kill oneanother. That is how I see it. And the result is that whichever of them is killed the loss is as great to Europe and to me.

In 1914 I was as sorry for the young Germans who lay slain and mutilated in No Man's Land as for the British lads who lay beside them, so I got no emotional satisfaction out of the war. It was to me a sheer waste of life. I am not forgetting the gratification that war gives to the instinct of pugnacity and admiration of courage that are so strong in women. In the old days when people lived in forests like gorillas or in caves like bears, a woman's life and that of her children depended on the courage and killing capacity of her mate. To this day in Abyssinia a Danakil woman will not marry a man until he proves that he has at least four homicides to his credit. In England on the outbreak of war civilized young women rush about handing white feathers to all young men who are not in uniform. This, like other survivals from savagery, is quite natural, but our women must remember that courage and pugnacity are not much use against machine guns and poison gas.

The pacifist movement against war takes as its charter the ancient document called the Sermon on the Mount, which is almost as often quoted as the speech which Abraham Lincoln is supposed to have delivered on the battlefield of Gettysburg. The sermon is a very moving exhortation, and it gives you one first-rate tip, which is to do good to those who despitefully use you and persecute you. I, who am a much hated man, have been doing that all my life, and I can assure you that there is no better fun, whereas revenge and resentment make life miserable and the avenger hateful. But such a command as 'Love oneanother', as I see it, is a stupid refusal to accept the facts of human nature. Why, are we lovable animals? Do you love the rate collector? Do you love Mr Lloyd George, and, if you do, do you love Mr Winston Churchill? Have you an all-embracing affection for Messrs Mussolini, Hitler, Franco, Atatürk, and the Mikado?[48] I do not like all these gentlemen, and even if I did how could I offer myself to them as a delightfully lovable person? I find

I cannot like myself without so many reservations that I look forward to my death, which cannot now be far off, as a good riddance. If you tell me to be perfect as my Father in heaven is perfect, I can only say that I wish I could. That would be more polite than telling you to go to the Zoo and advise the monkeys to become men and the cockatoos to become birds of paradise. The lesson we have to learn is that our dislike for certain persons, or even for the whole human race, does not give us any right to injure our fellow creatures, however odious they may be.

As I see it, the social rule must be 'Live and let live,' and people who break this rule persistently must be liquidated. The pacifists and non-resisters must draw a line accordingly. When I was a young man in the latter half of the nineteenth century war did not greatly concern me personally because I lived on an island far away from the battlefield, and because the fighting was done by soldiers who had taken up that trade in preference to any other open to them. Now that aeroplanes bring battle to my housetop, and governments take me from my proper work and force me to be a soldier whether I like it or not, I can no longer regard war as something that does not concern me personally. You may say that I am too old to be a soldier. If nations had any sense they would begin a war by sending their oldest men into the trenches. They would not risk the lives of their young men except in the last extremity. In 1914 it was a dreadful thing to see regiments of lads singing Tipperary[49] on their way to the slaughterhouse, but the spectacle of regiments of octogenarians hobbling to the front waving their walking sticks and piping up to the tune of 'We'll never come back no more, boys, we'll never come back no more,'[50] wouldnt you cheer that enthusiastically? I should. But let me not forget that I should be one of them.

It has become a commonplace to say that another great war would destroy civilization. Well, that will depend on what sort of war it will be. If it is to be like the 1914 war, a war of nations, it will certainly not make an end of civilization. It may conceivably knock the British Empire to bits and leave England as primitive as she was when Julius Caesar landed in Kent. Perhaps we shall be happier then, for we are still savages at heart, and wear our thin uniform of civilization very awkwardly. But, anyhow, there will be two refuges left for civilization. No national attack can seriously hurt the two great federated republics of North America and Soviet Russia. They are too big. The distances are too great. But what could destroy them is civil war – wars like the wars of religion in the seventeenth century – and this is exactly the sort of war that is threatening us today. It has already begun in Spain, where all the big capitalist powers are taking a hand to support General Franco through an intervention committee which they think it more decent to call a Non-Intervention Committee. This is only a skirmish in the class war, the war between the two religions of capitalism and communism, which is at bottom a war between labor and land owning. We could escape that war by putting our house in order as Russia has done, without any of the fighting and killing and waste and damage that the Russians went through. But we dont seem to want to. I have shewn exactly how it can be done, and in fact how it must be done, but nobody takes any notice. Foolish people in easy circumstances flatter themselves that there is no such thing as the class war in the British Empire, where we are all far too respectable and too well protected by our Parliamentary system to have any vulgar unpleasantness of that sort. They deceive themselves. We are up to the neck in class war. What is it that is wrong with our present way of doing things? It is not that we cannot produce enough goods; our machines turn out as much work in an hour as ten thousand hand workers used to. But it is not enough for a country to produce goods. It must distribute them as well, and this is where our system breaks down hopelessly. Everybody ought to be living quite comfortably by working four or five hours a day with two Sundays in the week. Yet millions of laborers die in the workhouse or on the dole after sixty years of hard toil so that a few babies may have hundreds of thousands a year before they are born. As I see it, this is not a thing to be argued about or to take sides about. It is stupid and wicked on the face of it, and it will smash us and our civilization if we do not resolutely reform it. Yet we do nothing but keep up a perpetual ballyhoo about Bolshevism, Fascism, Communism, Liberty, Dictators, Democracy, and all the rest of it. The very first lesson of the new history dug up for us by Professor Flinders Petrie[51] during my lifetime is that no civilization, however splendid, illustrious, and like our own, can stand up against the social resentments and class conflicts which follow a silly misdistribution of wealth, labor, and leisure. And it is the one history lesson that is never taught in our schools, thus confirming the saying of the German philosopher Hegel: 'We learn from history that men never learn anything from history.'[52] Think it over.

'Theatres in Time of War' (1939)

Shaw's letter to The Times *was published 5th September 1939. Theatres were closed from 4th to 19th September 1939. Thereafter, some theatres re-opened, often staging lunchtime or early evening performances.*

May I be allowed to protest vehemently against the order to close all theatres and picture-houses during the war? It seems to me a masterstroke of unimaginative stupidity.

During the last War we had 80,000 soldiers on leave to amuse every night. There were not enough theatres for them; and theatre rents rose to fabulous figures. Are there to be no theatres for them this time? We have hundreds of thousands of evacuated children to be kept out of mischief and traffic dangers. Are there to be no pictures for them?

The authorities, now all-powerful, should at once set to work to provide new theatres and picture-houses where these are lacking.

All actors, variety artists, musicians, and entertainers of all sorts should be exempted from every form of service except their own all-important professional one.

What agent of Chancellor Hitler is it who has suggested that we should all cower in darkness and terror 'for the duration'?

'Why, brother soldiers, why
Should we be melancholy, boys?'[53]

'Uncommon Sense About the War' (1939)

Shaw's article was published in The New Statesman, *7th October 1939. An editorial note declared: 'Manifestly, we are not to be taken as endorsing the views expressed' by Shaw's 'provocative contribution'.*

The war in Poland is over. Every person in the country capable of seeing three moves ahead in the game of military chess has known this from the moment when the first Russian soldier stepped across the Polish frontier. Poland surrendered and laid herself at Herr Hitler's feet. He was able to say that as Poland's cause is lost we have no further excuse for continuing the war. Whereupon we threw off the mask of knight errantry and avowed flatly that we did not care two hoots about Poland and were out, on our old balance of power lines, to disable Germany, which we now called abolishing Hitlerism.

This left the Führer in a very dangerous position. The Axis had broken in his hands from the beginning, Italy and Spain having promptly deserted him. The anti-Comintern Pact[54] had become a danger to him. Turkey was definitely against him: Rumania and the Balkans generally were mortally afraid of him. America's neutrality was pro-British just as our non-intervention policy in the Spanish war was pro-Franco. 1918 had proved that Germany, though unconquerable and even victorious here and there in the field, could be starved into complete demoralisation and defeat by the Allies. The situation was not pleasant even for a leader drunk with success. The encirclement was fairly complete.

Except on one side, where Russia stood with an army of six million men eating their heads off. Those of us who were intelligent and knowledgeable enough to see that the balance of power was in the hands of Stalin had forced our Government to make overtures to Russia, and Mr Duff Cooper,[55] a very favourable specimen of our reigning oligarchy, loosened his old school tie so far as to plead in *The Evening Standard* that Stalin, though of course a blood-thirsty scoundrel, was perhaps not quite so villainous as Hitler. Herr Hitler, having the tremendous advantage over Mr Duff Cooper of being a proletarian and knowing something about the world he was living in, courted Russia more sensibly.

Stalin, five hundred per cent. or so abler and quicker at the uptake than all the dictators, including the Westminster Cabinet, rolled into one, had nothing to consider except which of them he should take by the scruff of the neck. Before deciding, he sent a handful of his six millions to take possession of White Russia, the Ukraine, and a substantial bit of Poland. Herr Hitler at once capitulated unconditionally, and was duly taken by the scruff of his neck; for Stalin could use Herr Hitler to keep Duff Cooperism out of the rest of Poland. He informed us in effect that since we could not even be civil to Russia we should not make Poland a gun emplacement for the obvious ultimate aim of our rulers (as far as they are capable of aims) of restoring the Romanoff Tsardom and once more dining happily with the Benkendorffs in Chester Square. And so the diplomatic situation stands. Nothing has happened since except that the French, whether after consultation with us or not I do not know, have most inopportunely started persecuting their Communists.

Meanwhile we are enduring all the vagaries, from mere discomfort to financial ruin and the breaking up of our homes, of the ineptest Military Communism. Powers which no Plantagenet king or Fascist dictator would dream of claiming have been granted to any unqualified person who offered to assume them, including an enterprising burglar. Whatever our work in life may be, we have been ordered to stop doing it and stand by. Wherever our wives and children are they have been transported to somewhere else, with or without the mothers. Our theatres and cinemas have been closed; and our schools, colleges and public libraries occupied by the military bureaucracy. We have been bundled out of our hotels into the streets neck and crop, and our own houses simultaneously made into nests of billeted little evacuees, often unofficially described as little hooligans. Our bungalows, bought by us after a careful calculation of our ability to pay the mortgage interest and get to our place of business in a Baby Austin,[56] have been put quite beyond our means by an appalling Budget, and by a rationing of petrol which aims at our complete immobilisation just as the blacking-out aims at our being completely blindfolded from sunset to sunrise. When the bungalows and suburbs raise a bitter cry that they cannot pay the new taxes, Sir John Simon[57] replies frankly that if they do not the Government will be forced to resort to inflation, thus reminding us that in Germany, when we forced the Reich to resort to it, a twopenny-halfpenny postage stamp cost £12,000, and the postman's wage rose to a king's ransom on which he could barely live, whilst annuities and insurances, on which unmarried elderly daughters and retired folk used to live in decency and comfort, became worthless. Our incomes depreciated from week to week through the rise in prices which the Government is pledged to prevent and cannot.

Such (and much more) is Military Communism in inexperienced hands, often the hands of fools who come to the top in wartime by their self-satisfied folly though nobody would trust them to walk a puppy in peace time. When we complain we are told that we must all make sacrifices, and that we had better buy white coats, carry our gas masks everywhere, and take wildly impracticable precautions against high explosive blast and poison gas.

Naturally we cry 'Sacrifice! Yes: but what for?' You tell us to be resolute and determined; but we cannot be resolute and determined in the air about nothing. What are we suffering for? Upon what are we resolved? What have we determined? What in the devil's name is it all about now that we have let Poland go?

Mr Chamberlain,[58] in reply, states our aim in a peroration. Mr Winston Churchill echoes it in a broadcast with a certain sense of its absurdity which the microphone betrays. Our aim is first to deliver Europe from the threat and fear of war. And our remedy is to promise it three years more war! Next, to abolish Hitlerism, root and branch. Well, what about beginning by abolishing Churchillism, a proposition not less nonsensical and more easily within our reach? But, we are told, if we do not send Hitler to St Helena,[59] he will proceed to annex Switzerland, Holland, Belgium, England, Scotland, Ireland, Australia, New Zealand, Canada, Africa, and finally the entire universe and Stalin will help him. I must reply that men who talk like this are frightened out of their wits. Stalin will see to it that nobody, not even our noble selves, will do anything of the sort; and Franklin Roosevelt[60] will be surprised to find himself exactly of Stalin's opinion in this matter. Had we not better wait until Herr Hitler tries to do it, and then stop him with Stalin and Roosevelt at our back?

The Archbishop of York,[61] in the next broadcast, rose finally to the occasion as became a great Christian prelate. Unfortunately he began not as a Christian prelate but as a righteously angry hotheaded Englishman by giving his blessing to our troops as 'dedicated' to the supreme immediate duty of lynching Herr Hitler and his associates. Now I cannot go into the question whether Herr Hitler deserves to be lynched without raising awkward analogies between his case and those of Signor Mussolini, General Franco, Stalin and his associates, and raking up events in India and Ireland which unfriendly pens have represented as somewhat dictatorial on our part. I simply remind the Archbishop that though we can easily kill a hundred thousand quite innocent Germans, man, woman and child, in our determination to get at

Herr Hitler, we should not finally succeed in lynching him; and the killing of the Germans, and our own losses in the process, would produce a state of mind on both sides which would operate as a complete black-out of Christianity and make the Archbishop's sane final solutions impossible. If we won, it would be Versailles over again,[62] only worse, with another war even less than twenty years off. And if, as is desperately possible, we drove Russia and Germany into a combination against us to avert that catastrophe, which is just what our Stalinphobe, Old School Ties and Trade Unionists are recklessly trying to do, then we shall indeed need God's help and not deserve it.

No: it will not do, however thickly we butter it with bunk and balderdash about Liberty, Democracy and everything we have just abolished at home. As the Archbishop nobly confesses, we made all the mischief, we and the French, when we were drunk with victory at Versailles; and if that mischief had not been there for him to undo Adolf Hitler would have now been a struggling artist of no political account. He actually owes his eminence to us; so let us cease railing at our own creation and recognise the ability with which he has undone our wicked work, and the debt the German nation owes him for it. Our business now is to make peace with him and with all the world instead of making more mischief and ruining our people in the process.

I write without responsibility, because I represent nobody but myself and a handful of despised and politically powerless intellectuals capable of taking a catholic view of the situation. One of these unhappy outcasts is my friend, H.G. Wells. He has written a vitally important letter to the *Times*, of which nobody has taken the smallest notice.[63] I disagree with him on one point, and would fain comfort him on it. He warns us that we are risking not merely military defeat, but the existence of civilisation and even of the human race. Dear H.G., let us not flatter ourselves. The utmost we can do is to kill, say, twenty-five millions of one another, and make the ruins of all our great cities show places for Maori tourists.

Well, let us. In a few months we shall all matter no more than last summer's flies. As two of the flies we naturally deprecate such an event; but the world will get on without us; and the world will have had an immense gratification of the primitive instinct that is at the bottom of all this mischief and that we never mention: to wit pugnacity, sheer pugnacity for its own sake, that much admired quality of which an example has just been so strikingly set us by the Irish Republican Army.[64]

'The Unavoidable Subject' (1940)

Shaw's BBC talk was scheduled to be broadcast in June 1940, but it was cancelled. This extract formed the second half of the talk.

The people still ask, What exactly is the Big Idea that we must risk our lives for?

Until our people get a clear answer they will not know where we stand against the German legions and the Fifth Column.

What makes it so puzzling is that nine-tenths of what Mr Hitler says is true. Nine-tenths of what Sir Oswald Mosley says is true.[65] Quite often nine-tenths of what our parliamentary favorites say to please us is emotional brag, bunk, and nonsense. If we start hotheadedly contradicting everything Mr Hitler and Sir Oswald say, we shall presently find ourselves contradicting ourselves very ridiculously, and getting the worst of the argument. We must sift out the tenth point for which we are fighting, and nail the enemy to that.

Let us come down to brass tacks. What am I, a superannuated non-combatant, encouraging young men to fight against? It is not German national socialism: I was a National Socialist before Mr Hitler was born. I hope we shall emulate and surpass his great achievement in that direction. I have no prejudices against him personally; much that he has written and spoken echoes what I myself have written and spoken. He has adopted even my diet. I am interested in him as one of the curiosities of political history; and I fully appreciate his physical and moral courage, his diplomatic sagacity, and his triumphant rescue of his country from the yoke the Allies imposed on it in 1918. I am quite aware of the fact that his mind is a twentieth-century mind, and that our governing class is mentally in the reign of Edward the Third, six centuries out of date. In short, I can pay him a dozen compliments which I could not honestly pay to any of our present rulers.

My quarrel with him is a very plain one. I happen to be what he calls a Nordic. In stature, in color, in length of head, I am the perfect blond beast whom Mr Hitler classes as the salt of the earth, divinely destined to rule over all lesser breeds. Trace me back as far as you can; and you will not find a Jew in my ancestry. Well, I have a friend who is a Jew. His name is Albert Einstein; and he is a far greater human prodigy than Mr Hitler and myself rolled into one. The nobility of his character has made his genius an unmixed benefit to his fellow creatures. Yet Adolf Hitler would compel me, the Nordic Bernard Shaw, to insult Albert Einstein; to claim moral superiority to him and unlimited power over him; to rob him, drive him out of his house, exile him, be punished if I allow a relative of mine to marry a relative of his; and finally to kill him as part of a general duty to exterminate his race. Adolf has actually done these things to Albert, bar the killing, as he carelessly exiled him first and thus made the killing impossible. Since then he has extended the list of reprobates from Semites to Celts and from Poles to Slavs; in short, to all who are not what he calls Nordics and Nazis. If he conquers these islands he will certainly add my countrymen, the Irish, to the list, as several authorities have maintained that the Irish are the lost tribes of Israel.

Now, this is not the sort of thing that sane men can afford to argue with. It is on the face of it pernicious nonsense; and the moment any ruler starts imposing it on his nation or any other nation by physical force there is nothing for it but for the sane men to muster their own physical forces and go for him. We ought to have declared war on Germany the moment Mr Hitler's police stole Einstein's violin. When the work of a police force consists not of *suppressing* robbery with violence but actually *committing* it, that force becomes a recruiting ground for the most infernal blackguards, of whom every country has its natural-born share. Unless such agents are disciplined and controled, their heads are turned by the authority they possess as a State police; and they resort to physical torture as the easiest way to do their work and amuse themselves at the same time. How is that discipline and control to be maintained? Not by an autocrat, because, as Napoleon said when he heard about Nelson and Trafalgar, an autocrat cannot be everywhere. When his police get out of hand and give his prisons and concentration camps a bad name, he has to back them up because he cannot do without them, and thus he becomes their slave instead of their master.

And this reminds me that we must stop talking nonsense about dictators. Practically the whole business of a modern civilized country is run by dictators and people who obey their orders. We call them bosses; but their powers are greater than those of any political dictator. To prevent them abusing those powers we have Factory Acts which have made short work of our employers' liberty to sacrifice the nation's interests to their own. It is true that we cannot get on without dictators in every street; but we can impose on them a discipline and a code of social obligations that remind them continually that their authority is given to them for the benefit of the commonwealth and not for their private gain. Well, one of our aims in this war is to impose a stiff international Factory Act on Mr Hitler, one that will deal not with wages and hours of labor, but with the nature of the work done, for peace or war.

When I say that we must stop talking nonsense about the war what I mean is that we must be careful not to go on throwing words about that we do not understand. Could anything be more ridiculous than people who were terrified the other day when Sir William Beveridge very properly used the word 'Socialist' to describe our war organization?[66] They flooded the B.B.C. with letters asking whether all their property was going to be taken away from them. Whilst they were writing, the Government in two hours and twenty minutes placed the country under the most absolute Military Communism. Everything we possess – our properties, our liberties, our lives – now belong to our country and not to ourselves. To say a word against Socialism or Communism is now treason. Without them we should soon have no property or liberty at all, and would be lucky if we were alive. Therefore I beg you, if you must talk, to confine yourself to what the lawyers call vulgar abuse, which will relieve your feelings and hurt nobody. I hope you are too much of a gentleman (or a lady) to call the Germans swine; but if you want to blow off steam by calling Mr Hitler a bloodstained monster do so by all means: it wont hurt him, nor need you worry if it does. But be careful; if you call Stalin a bloodstained monster you must be shot as the most dangerous of Fifth Columnists; for the friendship of Russia is vitally important to us just now. Russia and America may soon have the fate of the world in their hands; that is why I am always so civil to Russia.

Remember that the really dangerous Fifth Column consists of the people who believe that Fascism is a better system of government than ours, and that what we call our democracy is a sham. They are not altogether wrong; but the remedy is for us to adopt all the good points of Fascism or Communism or any other Ism, not to allow Mr Hitler and his Chosen Race to impose it on us by his demoralized police. We are fighting him, not for his virtues, but for his persecutions and dominations, which have no logical connection whatever with Fascism and which I hope we will not put up with from Mr Hitler or anyone else. He is as sure that God is on his side as Lord Halifax[67] is that God is on ours. If so, then we shall have to fight God as well as Mr Hitler. But as most of us believe that God made both Mr Hitler and Lord Halifax, we must reasonably believe that God will see fair. And the rest is up to us.

Wartime Life in the Country (1940)

Shaw's letter to his friend, the Greek scholar Gilbert Murray (1866-1957), was written 23rd October 1940.

We are here in a village where there are no shelters, no fire brigade, no guns, nothing warlike except a searchlight and a little siren which explodes every ten minutes or so. As the raiders are highly scientific, and fly blindly by their instruments, they begin every night by bombarding us in the firm conviction that they are making direct hits on Churchill's hat when as a matter of fact they are missing mine by a mile or two and shaking the house to remind us that there is a war on and that we are all in the front line.

I began by being pigheaded and refusing to let them disturb my routine of 3½ days in the country and 3½ in town every week. This alarmed Providence for my safety. The day before the Blitz, as we were starting for town as usual, Charlotte fell and hurt her knees so badly that she had to be helped upstairs, and the journey to London was out of the question. She is well now; but the pigheadedness has been bombed out of us; and we havnt been up to Whitehall Court for seven weeks. We can see fireworks here from our windows, which is quite enough for us. Two of our windows and a door panel have been smashed by one of the 12 hits in the Whitehall district; but here we only get shaken. We console ourselves with the mathematical chances against our being hit; but the facts, as usual, ignore mathematics and strongly support the theory of a mystical human polarization by which some people attract bombs and torpedoes, and others repel them.

The village people all call the war senseless; but as they are as helpless as you and I there is nothing for it but fatalism, which the wireless calls our heroism, and a strong objection to allow Ittler [sic] to control our destinies. The childishness of the politicians is appalling. Churchill occasionally tells as much of the truth as he safely can over the wireless. Then he takes an audible gulp of his favorite stimulant and, with a preliminary yell, gives the gallery a peroration and denounces Nazi scoundrels who actually bomb civilians, women and children. He is immediately followed by the news announcer, who begins by describing how the R.A.F. has rained bombs on the railway stations of Berlin etc. etc. In a sardonic mood one can turn on the Rome Radio, or Haw Haw,[68] and listen to the news over again, with the names reversed, but the moral indignation an exact echo. But this poor amusement does not bear its daily repetition.

'Military and Non-Military Objectives' (1941)

Shaw's letter to The Times *was published 28th April 1941 and co-signed by Gilbert Murray. Their letter supported the proposal made by George Bell (1883–1958), Bishop of Chichester, in* The Times, *17th April 1941.*

First, may we make clear that though we are about to propose an arrangement with the Axis, it is not in the nature of an armistice or a statement of war aims or anything else that could be interpreted as a symptom of weakening on the part of the Allies. Nor is it a new departure. As a precedent we cite the dealings between our postal authorities and those of the enemy by which at last prisoners of war on both sides are receiving letters from home with certainty and regularity in three weeks after their date. This enormous improvement on the pre-existing state of things could not have been effected without negotiations which, if not precisely cordial, were governed by a reciprocal disposition to listen to reason and make a bargain benefiting the belligerents equally.

There are methods of warfare which not only cannot produce a decision but are positively beneficial to the side against which they are directed. The bombardment of cities from the air may be one of them. Its conditions are quite unprecedented. Both victory and defeat are impossible, because the vanquished cannot surrender, and the victor must run for home at 300 miles an hour, pursued by fighters at 400 miles an hour. The recent bombardments of Berlin and London, though quite successful as such, have not produced any military result beyond infuriating the unfortunate inhabitants. Some of them have been killed. If raids could be maintained nightly and each raid killed 1,000 persons, half of them women it would take over a century to exterminate us and a century and a half to exterminate the Germans. Meanwhile, as both sides are depending for victory on famine by blockade, the reduction in the number of civilian mouths to be fed would be a relief to us.

As to one specific course which the War Cabinet has been provoked into taking: to wit, the threat to demolish Rome if Athens or Cairo be attacked from the air, it forces us to ask whether Rome does not belong to the culture of the whole world far more than to the little Italian-speaking group of Benitos and Beppos who at present are its local custodians. By destroying it we should be spiting the noses to vex the faces of every educated person in the British Commonwealth and in America, to say nothing of the European mainland. We may smash it for the Italians; but who is to give it back to us? In Rome no one is a stranger and a foreigner: we all feel when we first go there that we are revisiting the scene of a former existence. As to the effect of the threat, surely the way to save Athens and Cairo is not to defy Herr Hitler to bombard them and thus make it a point of honour for him to reply by a shower of bombs on them. He, far from the seven hills, may even echo the late

Lord Clanricarde's reply to his Irish tenants, 'If you think you can intimidate me by shooting my agent you are very much mistaken.'[69]

That we should in the same breath indignantly deny that our last raid on Berlin was a reprisal, and announce a major reprisal which must have staggered the historical conscience of the world, shows that our heads are not as clear as they might be on this subject. The more we endeavour to think it out the more we find ourselves driven to the conclusion that whatever may be said from the military point of view for our treatment of Bremen, Hamburg, and Kiel, there is nothing to be said for the demolition of metropolitan cities as such, and that the Bishop of Chichester's plea for a reconsideration of that policy is entirely justified.

'The Atomic Bomb' (1945)

Shaw's letter to The Times *was published 20th August 1945. The United States dropped atomic bombs on Hiroshima and Nagasaki, Japan, on 6th and 9th August 1945.*

Now that we, the human race, have begun monkeying with the atom, may I point out one possible consequence that would end all our difficulties?

For some years past our too few professional astronomers have been reinforced by a body of amateurs whose main activity is the watching and study of the variable stars. They have been excited several times by the sudden flaming up of what they call a new star, though it is in fact an old star, too small and cool to be visible, which has suddenly burst and blown up, leaving nothing but a cloud of star dust called a nebula. The heat energy liberated in the explosion is beyond human apprehension.

Apparently what has happened to these stars, and may happen to this earth of ours, is that the protons with their planetary electrons, and the heavier planetless neutrons of which their matter is composed, have combined, and produced a temperature at which the whole star has pulverized and evaporated, and its inhabitants, if any, have been cremated with an instantaneous thoroughness impossible at Golders Green.[70]

What we have just succeeded in doing at enormous expense is making an ounce of uranium explode like the star. The process, no longer experimental, will certainly be cheapened; and at any moment heavier elements than uranium, as much more explosive than uranium as uranium than gunpowder, may be discovered.

Finally, like the sorcerer's apprentice, we may practise our magic without knowing how to stop it, thus fulfilling the prophecy of Prospero.[71] In view of our behaviour recently, I cannot pretend to deprecate such a possibility; but I think it is worth mentioning.

Geneva, Preface (1945)

Geneva *was performed in 1938 at the Malvern Festival and then in London. During its successful London run Shaw continued to revise the play in order to reflect current events. This extract from Shaw's 1945 Preface is taken from the 1947 edition of the play.*

It was this improbability [of being killed in a specific air raid] which made pre-atomic air raiding futile as a means of intimidating a nation, and enabled the government of the raided nation to prevent the news of the damage reaching beyond its immediate neighborhood. One night early in the resumed war I saw, from a distance of 30 miles, London burning for three hours. Next morning I read in the newspapers that a bomb had fallen on the windowsill of a city office, and been extinguished before it exploded. Returning to London later on I found that half the ancient city had been levelled to the ground, leaving only

St Paul's and a few church towers standing. The wireless news never went beyond 'some damage and a few casualties in Southern England' when in fact leading cities and seaports had been extensively wrecked. All threatening news was mentioned only in secret sessions of parliament, hidden under heavy penalties until after the victory. In 1941, after the Dunkirk rout,[72] our position was described by the Prime Minister to the House of Commons in secret session as so desperate that if the enemy had taken advantage of it we should have been helplessly defeated; and it is now the fashion to descant dithyrambically on the steadfast heroism with which the nation faced this terrible emergency. As a matter of fact the nation knew nothing about it. Had we been told, the Germans would have overheard and rushed the threatened invasion they were bluffed into abandoning. Far from realizing our deadly peril, we were exulting in the triumph of our Air Force in 'the Battle of Britain' and in an incident in South America in which three British warships drove one German one into the river Plate.[73] Rather than be interned with his crew the German captain put to sea again against hopeless odds; scuttled his ship; and committed suicide. The British newspapers raved about this for weeks as a naval victory greater than Salamis, Lepanto, and Trafalgar rolled into one...[74]

All this was necessary and inevitable. It was dangerous to tell the truth about anything, even about the weather. The signposts on the roads had to be taken down and hidden lest they should help an invader to find his way. It was a crime to give an address with a date, or to scatter a few crumbs for the birds. And it was an act of heroic patriotism to drop a bomb weighing ten thousand pounds on dwellings full of women and children, or on crowded railway trains. Our bombing of foreign cities not only in Germany but in countries which we claimed to be 'liberating' became so frightful that at last the word had to be given to two of our best broadcasters of war reports to excuse them on the ground that by shortening the war they were saving the lives of thousands of British soldiers.

Meanwhile nobody noticed how completely war, as an institution, had reduced itself to absurdity. When Germany annexed Poland in 1939, half of it was snatched out of her jaws by Soviet Russia. The British Commonwealth having bound itself to maintain inviolate the frontiers of Poland as they were left after the fighting of 1914–18 with a Polish corridor cut right through Prussia to the Baltic, was committed to declare war on Germany and Russia simultaneously. But the British people and their rulers were in no mood to black out their windows and recommence the Four Years War in defence of this distant and foreign corridor. Being, as usual, unprepared for war, we tried to appease Germany and yet keep the peace with Soviet Russia...

It happened that in Munich in 1930 there was a young man named Hitler who had served in the Four Years War. Having no special military talent he had achieved no more as a soldier than the Iron Cross and the rank of corporal. He was poor and what we call no class, being a Bohemian with artistic tastes but neither training nor talent enough to succeed as an artist, and was thus hung up between the bourgeoisie for which he had no income and the working class for which he had no craft. But he had a voice and could talk, and soon became a beer cellar orator who could hold his audience. He joined a cellar debating society (like our old Cogers Hall) and thereby brought its numbers up to seven. His speeches soon attracted considerable reinforcements and established him as a leading spirit. Much of what he spouted was true. As a soldier he had learnt that disciplined men can make short work of mobs; that party parliaments on the British model neither could nor would abolish the poverty that was so bitter to him; that the Treaty of Versailles under which Germany, defeated and subjected far beyond the last penny she could spare, could be torn up clause by clause by anyone with a big enough army to intimidate the plunderers; and that Europe was dominated economically by a plutocracy of financiers who had got the whip hand even of the employers. So far he was on solid ground, with unquestionable facts to support him. But he mixed the facts up with fancies such as that all plutocrats are Jews; that the Jews are an accursed race who should be exterminated as such; that the Germans are a chosen race divinely destined to rule the world; and that all she needs to establish her rule is an irresistible army. These delusions were highly flattering to Hans, Fritz, and Gretchen at large as well as to the beer drinkers in the cellar; and when an attempt was made to silence the new Hitlerites by hired gangsters, Hitler organized a bodyguard for himself so effectively that the opposition was soon sprawling in the street.

With this stock in trade Hitler found himself a born leader, and, like Jack Cade, Wat Tyler, Essex under Elizabeth Tudor, Emmet under Dublin Castle,[75] and Louis Napoleon under the Second Republic, imagined he had only to appear in the streets with a flag to be acclaimed and followed by the whole population...

So far he was the creature and tool of the plutocracy. But the plutocracy had made a bad bargain. The moment it made Hitler a figure head, popular idolatry made a prophet and a hero of him, and gave him a real personal power far in excess of that enjoyed by any commercial magnate. He massacred all his political rivals not only with impunity but with full parliamentary approval. Like St Peter on a famous earlier occasion the German people cried 'Thou art the Christ,' with the same result. Power and worship turned Hitler's head; and the national benefactor who began by abolishing unemployment, tearing up the Treaty of Versailles, and restoring the selfrespect of sixty millions of his fellow countrymen, became the mad Messiah who, as lord of a Chosen Race, was destined to establish the Kingdom of God on earth – a German kingdom of a German God – by military conquest of the rest of mankind. Encouraged by spineless attempts to appease him he attacked Russia, calculating that as a crusader against Soviet Communism he would finally be joined by the whole Capitalist West.

But the Capitalist West was much too shortsighted and jealous to do anything so intelligent. It shook hands with Stalin and stabbed Hitler in the back. He put up a tremendous fight, backed by his fellow adventurers in Italy and Spain; but, being neither a Julius Caesar nor a Mahomet, he failed to make his initial conquests welcome and permanent by improving the condition of the inhabitants. On the contrary he made his name execrated wherever he conquered. The near West rose up against him, and was joined by the mighty far West of America. After twelve years of killing other people he had to kill himself, and leave his accomplices to be hanged.

The moral for conquerors of empires is that if they substitute savagery for civilization they are doomed. If they substitute civilization for savagery they make good, and establish a legitimate title to the territories they invade. When Mussolini invaded Abyssinia[76] and made it possible for a stranger to travel there without being killed by the native Danakils he was rendering the same service to the world as we had in rendering by the same methods (including poison gas) in the north west provinces of India, and had already completed in Australia, New Zealand, and the Scottish Highlands. It was not for us to throw stones at Musso, and childishly refuse to call his puppet king Emperor. But we did throw stones, and made no protest when his star was eclipsed and he was scandalously lynched in Milan. The Italians had had enough of him; for he, too, was neither a Caesar nor a Mahomet...

Meanwhile here we are, with our incompetence armed with atomic bombs. Now power civilizes and develops mankind, though not without having first been abused to the point of wiping out entire civilizations. If the atomic bomb wipes out ours we shall just have to begin again. We may agree on paper not to use it as it is too dangerous and destructive; but tomorrow may see the discovery of that poisonous gas lighter than air and capable before it evaporates through the stratosphere of killing all the inhabitants of a city without damaging its buildings or sewers or water supplies or railways or electric plants. Victory might then win cities if it could repopulate them soon enough, whereas atomic bombing leaves nothing for anyone, victor or vanquished. It is conceivable even that the next great invention may create an overwhelming interest in pacific civilization and wipe out war. You never can tell.[77]

'Nuremberg' (1946)

Shaw's letter to The Times *was published 21st October 1946.*

Among the insanities that war always produces should be classed the general assumption that the suicide of Göring has been a defeat for the Nuremberg tribunal[78] and the victorious Powers, and that the most rigorous inquiry must be made as to who connived at it by some relaxation of the manacling and spyhole inspection to which the prisoner was subjected. One would suppose that his evasion of the rope threatens us with a third world war.

This is not how it strikes me; and it is because I believe that my feeling is not altogether unrepresentative that I venture to ask you to make it known. Had the matter been in my hands I should have supplied all the condemned men with a liberal supply of morphia tablets and given them every opportunity of sparing us the disgusting job of hanging them.

Farfetched Fables (1948–9)

In the first fable, a Young Man and Young Woman meet casually in 'a public park on a fine summer afternoon'.

YOUNG MAN Ive got into this conversation with a view to our possible marriage.

YOUNG WOMAN Nothing doing. I'll not marry.

YOUNG MAN It is odd that so many attractive women are unmarried. Dull ugly frumps never seem to have any difficulty in finding mates. Why wont you marry? I am available.

YOUNG WOMAN My father was shot in the Great War that now seems such a little one. My eldest brother was killed in Normandy when we were liberating France there. His wife and children were blown to bits by a bomb that wrecked the whole street they lived in. Do you think I'll bear children for that?

YOUNG MAN They died for England. They made war to end war. Dont you admire bravery? Dont you love your country?

YOUNG WOMAN What use is bravery now when any coward can launch an atomic bomb? Until men are wise and women civilized they had better not be born. At all events I shall not bring them into this wicked world to kill and be killed.

An excited middle-aged man comes along waving a newspaper and cheering.

M.A.M. Hurrah! Have you heard the news?

YOUNG MAN No. Whats happened?

M.A.M. No more war. The United Nations have abolished it.

YOUNG MAN [*disparagingly*] Hmm! May I have a look at your paper?

M.A.M. Here it is in black and white. You may keep it. I'll buy another. Hurrah! hurrah!! hurrah!!!

He hands over the paper and rushes away, cheering.

YOUNG WOMAN What does it say?

YOUNG MAN [*reading the headlines*] 'THE WORLD AT PEACE AT LAST. WASHINGTON AGREES. MOSCOW AGREES. CHINA AGREES. THE WESTERN UNION AGREES. THE FEDERALISTS AGREE. THE COMMUNISTS AGREE. THE FASCISTS AGREE. ATOMIC BOMB MANUFACTURE MADE A CAPITAL CRIME. UNIVERSAL SECURITY GUARANTEED.'

YOUNG WOMAN Have the armies been disbanded? Have the military academies been closed? Has conscription been abolished?

YOUNG MAN It doesnt say. Oh yes: here is a stop press paragraph. 'ARMIES WILL IN FUTURE BE CALLED WORLD POLICE. NO MORE CONSCRIPTION.' Hm!

YOUNG WOMAN You dont seem pleased.

YOUNG MAN I dont swallow all that rot about no more war. Men will always fight even if they have nothing to fight with but their fists. And the women will egg them on.

YOUNG WOMAN What does the leading article say?

YOUNG MAN [*turning to the leader page and quoting*] 'Truce of God begins a new chapter in the history of the globe. The atomic bomb has reduced war to absurdity; for it threatens not only both victors and vanquished but the whole neutral world. We do not as yet know for certain that the bomb that disintegrated Hiroshima is not still at work disintegrating. The weather has been curiously unusual ever since. But no nation will ever venture on atomic warfare again.'

YOUNG WOMAN Do you believe that?

YOUNG MAN Yes; but it wont stop war. In 1914 the Germans tried poison gas; and so did we. But the airmen who dropped it on the cities could not stay in the air for long; and when they had to come down they found the streets full of the gas, because poison gas is heavier than air and takes many days to disperse. So in the last war gas was not used; and atomic bombs wont be used in the next one.

YOUNG WOMAN Oh! So you think there will be a next one.

YOUNG MAN Of course there will, but not with atomic bombs. There is no satisfaction in seeing the world lit up by a blinding flash, and being burnt to dust before you have time to think about it, with every stick and stone for miles around falling and crumbling, all the drains and telephones and electrics torn up and flung into the air, and people who are too far off to be burnt die of radiation. Besides, bombs kill women. Killing men does not matter: the women can replace them; but kill the women and you kill the human race.

YOUNG WOMAN That wont stop war. Somebody will discover a poison gas lighter than air! It may kill the inhabitants of a city; but it will leave the city standing and in working order.

YOUNG MAN [*thoughtfully, letting the newspaper drop on his knees*] That is an idea.

YOUNG WOMAN What idea?

YOUNG MAN Yours. There is a lot of money in it. The Government gave £100,000 to the man who found out how to land our army in Normandy in 1945.

YOUNG WOMAN Governments will pay millions for any new devilment, though they wont pay twopence for a washing machine. When a Jewish chemist found out how to make high explosive cheaply we made him a present of Jerusalem, which didnt belong to us.

YOUNG MAN [*hopefully*] Yes, by George! So we did.

YOUNG WOMAN Well, what of it?

YOUNG MAN I'm a chemist.

YOUNG WOMAN Does that mean that you are in the atomic bomb business?

YOUNG MAN No; but I'm on the staff in a chlorine gas factory. The atomic bomb people may be barking up the wrong tree.

YOUNG WOMAN [*rising wrathfully*] So that is what you are! One of these scientific devils who are destroying us! Well, you shall not sit next me again. Go where you belong: to hell. Good day to you.

She goes away.

YOUNG MAN [*still thoughtful*] Lighter than air, eh? [*Slower*] Ligh–ter–than–air?

The scene fades out.

In the second fable, the population of the Isle of Wight is killed by a new volatile gas, as is its inventor.

'Atomic Welfare' (1949)

Shaw's letter to The Times *was published 24th December 1949.*

Much of your space and time is being wasted on the subject of atomic warfare. The disuse of poison gas in the 1939–45 war because it was as dangerous to its users as to their targets, makes it very unlikely that atomic bombs will be used again. If they are they will promptly make an end of all our discussions by making an end of ourselves. Meanwhile, they are distracting attention from the far more vital and pressing subject of atomic welfare. Our present concern is with the threatened water shortage, which may leave us crying, like Coleridge's Ancient Mariner: 'Water, water, everywhere; and not a drop to drink.' This could be averted by distilling sea water, were it not that the cost of the necessary heat is greater than we can afford. Atom disintegration will some day make heat cheaper than can coal-burning. We shall carry in our pockets tiny pips, one of which dropped into a cup of water, will instantly make it boil. Such pips would be worth incalculably more than atomic bombs, which nobody would dare to use. I have no hope of any notice being taken of these potentialities any more than my old urgings that our monster tides change the old lay to 'Power, power, everywhere: and voltage minus one.' Still, give me space for another cry in the wilderness, that my unquiet spirit, wandering among the ruins of empires, may have at least the mean and melancholy satisfaction of saying: 'I told you so.'

Notes

1. The American civil war began on 12th April 1861.
2. Cecil Rhodes (1853–1902), a South African statesman, developed
land north of the Transvaal that was named Rhodesia (now Zimbabwe).
Joseph Chamberlain (1836–1914) was secretary for the British colonies
1895–1903.
3. Alfred Milner (1854–1925) was High Commissioner in South Africa
and surrounded himself with his 'kindergarten' of young Oxford graduates
to help him administer the country.
4. The Maxim machine gun was developed in the 1880s.
5. Kaiser Wilhelm II (1859–1941) of Prussia and Germany.
6. In his *The Perfect Wagnerite* (1898) Shaw quotes from Richard Wagner's
(1813–83) letter to his friend and fellow composer, August Röckel (1814–76):
'We must learn to die, and to die in the fullest sense of the word. The fear of
the end is the source of all lovelessness; and this fear is generated only when
love begins to wane.'
7. Tom Mann (1856–1941) was a prominent trade unionist who had been
imprisoned in 1911 for sedition; he opposed the war. Robert Blatchford
(1851–1943), sometime Fabian turned right-wing jingoist, was to attack
Common Sense as treachery.
8. The Charity Organisation Society was founded in 1869 to assist struggling
families and to coordinate the efforts of various charities.
9. Lord Horatio Herbert Kitchener (1850–1916), field marshal and
secretary of state for war, predicted the war would last at least three years,
kill countless soldiers, and be won by the side with the most soldiers.
10. The Brabançonne is the Belgian national anthem. Shaw plays on the
nursery rhyme, 'Pop goes the weasel.'
11. After the Franco-German war of 1870–1, the Treaty of Frankfurt (1871)
stipulated that France pay Germany reparations of five billion gold francs.
12. 'Blut is ein ganz besonderer Saft': blood is a very special juice
(Mephistopheles to Faust, in Goethe's *Faust*).
13. Friedrich Nietzsche (1844–1900). His superman, 'Übermensch',
in *Also sprach Zarathustra* (1883–5), is echoed strongly in Shaw's *Man
and Superman*.
14. At the Battle of Agincourt (25th October 1415) Henry V ordered
French prisoners killed when faced with another possible attack.
15. Carthage must be destroyed.
16. The seven weeks' Austro-Prussian war was settled with the Treaty
of Prague (1866); Prussia annexed Schleswig-Holstein and other
territories.

17. H.G. Wells (1866–1946), *The War of the Worlds* (1898); Anatole France (1844–1924), *Penguin Island* (1908).

18. Horatio Bottomley (1860–1933), Liberal M.P., founder in 1906 of the patriotic weekly, *John Bull*, and actively involved in recruiting solders.

19. On 25th May 1916 Labour Party leader Arthur Henderson (1863–1935) became President of the Board of Education.

20. You didn't mean it, Willy, eh?

21. Field Marshall Sir Douglas Haig (1861–1928).

22. H.W. Massingham (1860–1924) was editor successively of *The Star*, *The Daily Chronicle*, and *The Nation*.

23. C.E. Montague (1867–1928), journalist, novelist, and critic, who dyed his hair in order to enlist (at the age of forty-seven).

24. The Germans' defensive line in northeastern France, not breached until 1918.

25. Goethe was in the losing Battle of Valmy (1792) that pitted Prussia against revolutionary France. Although sympathetic to the rioters, Wagner fled the Dresden insurrection of 1849.

26. Three-inch mortars.

27. Shaw rephrases Genesis 4:10: 'The voice of thy brother's blood crieth unto me from the ground.'

28. Former viceroy of India from 1898–1905, George Nathaniel Curzon (1859–1925) served in the wartime coalition government and was later foreign secretary (1919–24).

29. Arthur James Balfour (1848–1930), former Prime Minister, and Foreign Secretary (1916–19).

30. Sir Roger Casement (1864–1916), Irish nationalist, who sought German assistance in the nationalist cause against Britain. Shaw wrote a defence for his trial, arguing Casement be treated as a prisoner of war. Casement declined to use it; he was hanged for treason.

31. After the Russo-Turkish war of 1877–8, Britain acquired Cyprus as part of the Treaty of Berlin (1878).

32. The Treaty of Limerick (1691) allowed James II's defeated forces to leave Ireland. Brian Boru (c.941–1014) was King of Ireland (1002–14).

33. The Irish Republican insurrection in central Dublin (April 1916) lasted one week; fifteen of its leaders were executed, including the commander James Connolly (1868–1916).

34. George Russell 'Æ' (1867–1935), Irish poet. James Larkin (1876–1947), Irish trade unionist, was imprisoned in 1920 for his Communist activities during the American 'Red Scare' period. The meeting, held in the Royal Albert Hall, London, on 1st November 1913, raised £410.

35. A career soldier, General Sir John Grenfell Maxwell (1859–1929) was Commander-in-Chief in Ireland during the Easter Rising.

36. Over 11,000 men were killed at the Battle of Neuve Chapelle (10–13th March 1915), and about 50,000 allied soldiers during the Gallipoli expedition (begun 25th April 1915).

37. The *Lusitania* was torpedoed on 7th May 1915. Among the drowned were: Charles Frohman (1856–1915), American theatre manager; Justus Miles Forman (1875–1915), American dramatist; Charles Klein (1867–1915), Anglo-American dramatist; and Sir Hugh Lane (1875–1915), Irish art collector.

38. The Battle of Festubert began on 15th May 1915; there were about 16,000 British casualties.

39. The naval Battle of Jutland took place in the North Sea on 31st May and 1st June 1916. Thereafter German ships were confined to port.

40. Edith Cavell (1865–1915) was a British nurse who, as matron of a Brussels hospital, helped 200 soldiers escape to the neutral Netherlands. Tried by the Germans, she was shot on 12th October 1915.

41. Poilu: hairy (a nickname for the French).

42. The Black and Tans were soldiers recruited after the war to supplement the Royal Irish Constabulary. Notoriously harsh, they were so nicknamed after the mixed colours of their uniforms.

43. In scene IV of *Saint Joan*, Peter Cauchon comments: 'I am no mere political bishop: my faith is to me what your honor is to you [Warwick]; and if there be a loophole through which this baptized child [Joan] of God can creep to her salvation, I shall guide her to it.'

44. The Fashoda incident (18th September 1898) in Egyptian Sudan (at present day Kodok) was the climax of a series of territorial disputes between Britain and France.

45. Austrian Archduke Franz Ferdinand was assassinated in Sarajevo on 28th June 1914.

46. Swift's *Gulliver's Travels* (1726), book 2, chapter 7.

47. The Spanish civil war (1936–9), the Sino-Japanaese war (1937–45).

48. These were all war-time leaders: David Lloyd George (1863–1945), Winston Churchill (1874–1965), Benito Mussolini (1883–1945), Adolf Hitler (1889–1945), Francisco Franco (1892–1975), Kemal Atatürk (1881–1938), Emperor Hirohito (1901–89).

49. The popular First World War song, 'It's a Long Way to Tipperary'.

50. 'We'll Never Come Back Any More, Boys,' is from a verse in Rudyard Kipling's (1865–1936) novel *The Light That Failed* (1890), chapter 14.

51. Professor Sir William Matthew Flinders Petrie (1853–1942), English Egyptologist.

52. See *The Philosophy of History* by Georg Wilhelm Friedrich Hegel (1770–1831), from his 1830–1 lectures, and first published 1837.

53. 'Why, soldiers, why' is a war song dating from 1729.

54. A 1936 agreement between Germany and Japan pledging hostility against international Communism that Italy joined in 1937. Broken in 1939 when Hitler signed the Nazi-Soviet pact.

55. Duff Cooper (1890–1954) had been Secretary of War (1935–7), and resigned from the government in 1938 because of its policy of appeasing of Hitler.

56. The original 'Baby' Austin 7 car was introduced in 1922.

57. Sir John Simon (1873–1954) was Chancellor of the Exchequer 1937–40.

58. Neville Chamberlain (1869–1940) became Prime Minister in 1937 and advocated the appeasement policy with Hitler. He resigned in 1940.

59. After his defeat at the Battle of Waterloo in 1815, Napoleon Bonaparte was exiled to the island of St Helena in the South Atlantic.

60. Franklin Delano Roosevelt (1882–1945), President of the United States (1933–45).

61. William Temple (1881–1944), Archbishop of York (1929–42), became Archbishop of Canterbury in 1942.

62. The Treaty of Versailles (1919) imposed heavy penalties on Germany.

63. Wells' letter published 26th September 1939 advocated candid discussion of war aims; otherwise, Wells foresaw 'no hope for mankind'.

64. The IRA had declared war on Britain in January 1939. Eire was a neutral country during the Second World War.

65. Sir Oswald Mosley (1896–1980) founded the British Union of Fascists in 1932 and was imprisoned 1940–3.

66. Sir William Beveridge (1879–1963), economist and social reformer; in 1942 he produced the Beveridge Report that laid the foundations of the modern welfare state.

67. Edward Frederick Wood, Lord Halifax (1881–1959) was Foreign Secretary (1938–40).

68. As 'Lord Haw Haw,' William Joyce (1904–46) broadcast German propaganda; he was hanged as a traitor.

69. Hubert George de Burgh Canning, marquess of Clanricarde (1832–1916), was a harsh Irish absentee landlord.

70. Shaw was cremated at Golders Green Crematorium, London, 6th November 1950.

71. 'The great globe itself, / Yea, all which it inherit, shall dissolve, / And, like this insubstantial pageant faded, / Leave not a rack behind' (Shakespeare, *The Tempest*, 4.1).

72. The British Expeditionary Force was evacuated from Dunkirk in May and June 1940.

73. The air Battle of Britain between Britain and Germany took place in July – October 1940. In December 1939, the German battleship *Graf Spee*, after sinking several ships, was driven by allied forces to the River Plate,

Montevideo, Uruguay; escape being impossible, the German captain blew up his ship.

74. Three great naval battles: Salamis (480 BC), Lepanto (1571), and Trafalgar (1805).

75. Jack Cade (d. 1450), rebel leader against Henry VI; Wat Tyler (d. 1381), leader of the Peasants' Revolt; the Earl of Essex (1541–76) attempted to subdue Ireland; and Robert Emmet (1778–1803), Irish nationalist, who led the unsuccessful 1803 uprising.

76. Italy invaded Abyssinia (Ethiopia) in October 1935.

77. Shaw's 'Pleasant Play' with this title was produced by the Stage Society in London in 1899.

78. The International Military Tribunal (1945–6) sentenced Hermann Göring (1893–1946), Hitler's loyal supporter and successor, to death; he committed suicide 15th October by taking poison.

Biographical note

Bernard Shaw was born in 1856 in Dublin. After only a short period of schooling and some time as a clerk in the land-agency office, he moved to London in 1876 to pursue a literary career. After a false start as a novelist, he found success in journalism, becoming art critic for *The World*, music critic (under the pseudonym 'Corno di Bassetto') for *The Star* and, from 1895 to 1898, theatre critic for *The Saturday Review*.

Shaw turned to playwriting with *Widowers' Houses*, first performed in 1892. His first commercial success, *Arms and the Man*, was produced in London and New York in 1894. Encouraged by the success of *The Devil's Disciple* in New York in 1897, he gave up most of his work as a critic. Other major works include *Man and Superman* (1903), *Major Barbara* (1905), *The Doctor's Dilemma* (1906), *Pygmalion* (1913) and *Saint Joan* (1923). He was awarded the Nobel Prize for Literature for 1925 and an Oscar for the screenplay of *Pygmalion* in 1939.

A passionate socialist, Shaw joined the newly formed Fabian Society in 1884, formulating the political theories of this group with Sidney Webb, writing and lecturing and eventually sitting on its executive committee. He also served as a borough councillor in St Pancras from 1897 to 1903.

In 1898 Shaw married Charlotte Payne-Townshend, and from 1905 they lived at what was to become known as Shaw's Corner in Ayot St Lawrence, Hertfordshire, until Charlotte's death in 1943 and Shaw's in 1950.

J.P. Wearing is Professor Emeritus of English, University of Arizona, and author of fifteen books including *Bernard Shaw and Nancy Astor*, *The Shakespeare Diaries: A Fictional Autobiography*, the sixteen-volume *The London Stage 1890–1959*, and critical editions of plays by Bernard Shaw and Arthur W. Pinero.